MANNY ALMEIDA'S RINGSIDE LOUNGE:

the cape verdeans' struggle for their neighborhood

Sam Beck

MANNY ALMEIDA'S RINGSIDE LOUNGE:

the Cape Verdeans' struggle for their neighborhood

Gávea-Brown

F89
.P99
C33
1992

Design
   Teófilo Ramos

Cover
   Christopher Dean

Published by
   Gávea-Brown Publications
   Department of Portuguese and Brazilian Studies
   Brown University
   Providence, Rhode Island 02912

Distributed by:
   Luso-Brazilian Books
   538 State Street
   Brooklyn, New York 11217

Library of Congress Catalog Card Number 92-72593

ISBN 0-943722-18-7

To my father Walter and my son Moisés

CONTENTS

Plates

Maps

FOREWORD

Ongoing physical and demographic change is an inevitable element in the life of any city. In America this is conceived of as an endless process of decay and renewal. In recent years it has often taken the form of gentrification. Old neighborhoods receive a physical overhaul through either replacement or renovation of existing structures. This is accompanied by a change in inhabitants. The poor are replaced by the more affluent and as often as not the poor are people of color and the affluent are not.

One of the many places where this has happened is in Fox Point, a neighborhood near Brown University in Providence, Rhode Island. In *Manny Almeida's Ringside Lounge*, Sam Beck gives us important insights into just how disruptive and painful gentrification can be for those who are forced out. From the vantage point of Manny's we learn who the old residents of the neighborhood were and how they reacted to the changes in their neighborhood. Beck shows us around Manny's, Dave's next door, and the rest of the Fox Point neighborhood, and introduces us to many of the people who lived there. He also takes us into Providence city offices and archives to show us how Fox Point came to be targeted for urban renewal and how the process played itself out.

Fox Point, we learn, was an ethnically mixed neighborhood with a strong Cape Verdean presence. These citizens of the United States came to this country from the Portuguese-speaking Cape Verde Islands, off the coast of Africa, in the nineteenth and twentieth centuries. They are people with a history, with a strong sense of cultural identity, and with the kind of social cohesion that lets Beck speak of them as a community in the best sense of the term.

We learn about the history of this community, about the shifting self-identity of the Cape Verdeans, and about Cape Verdeans' identification of Fox Point as their neighborhood. We learn how they struggled to maintain their identity as a community even after they had been forced out of Fox Point, and of how Manny's and a few other locations served as centers where the struggle was carried on.

As one reads Beck's narrative, a single question emerges as central: why isn't neighborhood renewal designed to improve the lives of the residents? The answer that emerges from this analysis is that profit, institutional expansion, and historic preservation take precedence over human relations and social well-being. In this instance, the continuing growth of nearby Brown University attracted new residents and upscale commercial establishments to Fox Point; affluent citizens wanted in-city housing; and developers, backed by city officials, saw ways to make money. The promotion of concern over urban decay and historic preservation created a political climate favorable to these goals.

The Fox Point Cape Verdeans caught the spirit of the process in referring to "urban renewal" as "nigger removal." Beck's analysis substantiates this characterization. No serious effort was made to discover who the residents of the neighborhood were and how their lives would be affected by the renewal projects. Instead, the physical appearance of the neighborhood and its residents, the former dilapidated and the latter Black, lent itself to an official view of Fox Point as a crime-ridden slum.

The official view was wrong and the gentrification process that it served to justify was unfair and unjust to the residents of Fox Point. For those who wish to live in a more fair and just society, the story is discouraging. At the same time, the telling of the story in print inspires hope. In the struggle to replace gentrification with renewal that can improve neighborhoods without destroying their communities, it will help to have a clear understanding of the problems that gentrification creates. *Manny Almeida's Ringside Lounge* is a significant step in that direction.

John W. Cole
Professor of Anthropology
University of Massachusetts, Amherst

14

Acknowledgments

The National Institute on Alcohol Abuse and Alcoholism, Social Science Research Training in Alcohol post-doctoral fellowship in the Brown University Department of Anthropology supported my work during a ten-month period in 1980-1981, under the directorship of Dr. Dwight B. Heath. I am grateful to the National Endowment for the Arts for funding public programs facilitating research about Cape Verdeans in Rhode Island in 1983 and 1984.

I am indebted to Marianne A. Cocchini, the former director of the Fox Point Community Organization, who encouraged me to start this project, provided me with space in which to complete the first draft of the book in 1981, and continued to encourage me to complete the book. I am grateful to Lilly Hoffman and Ira Katznelson of the New School for Social Research for reading and commenting on earlier drafts and to John W. Cole of the University of Massachusetts and Richard Lobban of Rhode Island College for extensive critiques that led to extensive revisions. Thanks to Michael Uhl and Beth Parkhurst who helped me edit the book. I took all their advice to heart, but did not always follow it in the recasting of subsequent drafts. I am also grateful to Steven Cabral, Carolyn Oliveira, Nonny Soars, members of the International Longshoremen's Union, and the countless number of Fox Point Cape Verdeans who attempted to make me understand the complexities of their history and lives. However much they influenced my work, I am responsible for errors of understanding, interpretation, and judgment in what is printed here.

I wish to offer a special note of thanks to Dean Margaret C. Jacob of Eugene Lang College, The New School for Social Research, for the subvention that made this publication possible, and to Onésimo Almeida of Brown University, who has been a patient and supportive publisher. Susan Savitzki provided me with word processing skills that helped bring this monograph to fruition.

Chapter 1

Introduction

This book explains the emergence, development, and decline of the Cape Verdean neighborhood of Fox Point in Providence, Rhode Island and the struggle by its members to retain their ethnic community identity. The vigorous expansion of Brown University, the implementation of longstanding government urban renewal policies, and the intensity of the historic preservation movement brought about the displacement of working poor from Fox Point in favor of real estate speculators who appealed to an urban-minded and upwardly mobile middle class. Such movements were precipitated in Providence by government and private investments in urban centers perjoratively designated as slums. In Fox Point such reinvestment brought two ideologies into conflict. Cape Verdeans saw Fox Point as *their* neighborhood and community, albeit a poor one. Developers (including governments) and investors perceived the properties there to have economic development potential that was being destroyed by the people who lived there. While each drew on history and moral imperatives to claim Fox Point as their own, the Cape Verdeans lost the struggle by ultimately being denied access to affordable housing and they were forced to witness their own dissipation as a community with longstanding ties to that neighborhood.

When I first arrived in Fox Point, I could not understand why people referred to the neighborhood as Cape Verdean. I asked myself, "If this was a Cape Verdean neighborhood, where did they come from and where did they go? Was it merely fortuitous that the displaced were primarily the Cape Verdeans who occupied the oldest and among the most dilapidated houses in Fox Point? Was it by chance that the neighborhood of Cape Verdeans was close to the desirable waterfront? Was it an accident that they were located in the area thought most suitable for highway construction, that brought to an end their close to one-hundred-year-old settlement? Was it a fluke that Manny Almeida's Ringside Lounge became the only Cape Verdean hangout in Fox Point, despite the visible absence of Cape Verdeans in the neighborhood?" I wanted to know, further, the nature of the relationship between Cape Verdeans and Manny's.

The research project occupied a period of eight months. I lived in the Fox Point community for six months and frequented Manny's on a daily basis. I spent much of my time speaking with the people who regularly came to Manny's and the restaurant next door, called "Dave's." I also frequented neighborhood streets, where I was able to meet people. I spent much time in the Fox Point Community Organization (FPCO), where some Cape Verdeans continued to work and remained active. As a participant-observer, I attempted to understand the perspective of the Cape Verdeans who frequented Manny Almeida's Ringside Lounge from their point of view, at times involving myself in their struggle against developers. I wanted to understand why they came to Manny's and why they claimed it to be their bar.

The more time I spent in Fox Point, the clearer the significance of my project became. Manny's was not just a place to drink, but a place where Cape Verdeans got together in what they called "their neighborhood" to share a common history and experience. It was also a place where Cape Verdeans could demonstrate a continued presence in their neighborhood. The fact that Cape Verdeans came to Manny's, then, became a critical link in my quest to discover their story and even something about their deeper identity.

My research was aided further by an analysis of documents, including the photographic collections of Cape Verdeans in the Rhode Island Historical Society Library, the Fox Point Community Organization videotape collection, urban-renewal-related materials of the Providence Urban Development Office, and the oral history collection located in the Rhode Island State Library Services. I carried out library research in the areas of Cape Verdean immigration, American immigration history, and the socioeconomic development history of Providence.

The oral accounts presented in Chapter 4 were gathered on the occasion of the fiftieth anniversary of Local 1329 of the International Longshoremen's Association over a three-week period in 1983, when I was invited by the union local to coordinate a commemoration program on the origins of this association (Beck 1983). At that time, I had the opportunity to interview the oldest members of the local longshoremen's union and close kin of Manuel Querino Ledo, a central figure in organizing dock workers in Providence. From 1981 through 1983, as an official of the City of Providence, Department of Public Parks, among other duties I was responsible for organizing and supporting Cape Verdean ethnic and folk arts festivals and events. In this capacity, I was able to develop my understanding of Cape Verdean Americans and gain a deeper view of the social context in which Fox Point Cape Verdeans lived (Cabral and Beck 1982).

In the process of working on my project, I found Cape Verdeans' behavior determined by their specific ethnicity in relationship to that of other cultural groups in Southeastern New England, on the one hand, and by their place within the socioeconomic hierarchy of the region, on the other. That is to say, I found that Cape Verdeans came to Manny's for reasons that had little to do with the pull of tradition. Frequenting Manny's was not habitual behavior, but had a subtle purpose that could be understood only by comprehending why Cape Verdeans claimed Manny Almeida's Ringside Lounge as their bar.

This discovery brought me to alter my approach from conventional anthropological methods that would have isolated Cape Verdeans by studying only their internal relations and culture trait complexes. Instead, I looked at the relationships between Cape Verdeans and other populations from a historical perspective. Rather than seeking out what defined Cape Verdean ethnicity, specific traits that made them distinctive, such as their foodways, social structure, rituals, or other sociocultural factors, I sought to discover the conditions that generated their ethnic group identity, reproduced it, transformed it, or brought it to decline. I sought to discover the process of ethnic identity development and change. Rather than looking only at boundary maintenance and development among ethnic groups in interaction, I looked at the conditions that brought them into interaction in the first place.

In order to explain why Cape Verdeans came to Manny's, I had to explain who the Cape Verdeans were, where they came from, and why they settled in Fox Point; I had to learn about Fox Point Cape Verdean identity development. Tracing such identity was not easy, since, as I proceeded, I discovered that the nature of their identity, as they told it to me and as it was recorded, changed over time and in relationship to changing contexts. I found not one Cape Verdean identity, but a number of them, and each had to be explained in turn.

Cape Verdeans settled in New England sometime in the second half of the nineteenth century. They had extensive contact with Yankee merchants and whalers. As they settled in Providence, they were drawn into a hierarchically integrated spatial arrangement in which social and economic status overlapped with statuses derived from their place in the production process, the color of their skin, and how recently they had immigrated to the United States. The unskilled, the "colored," and those who had most recently immigrated entered society on its bottom rung.

The arrangement of the chapters represents a periodization schema in which the contexts of Fox Point Cape Verdean ethnic group identity crystallized as a political force. Chapter 2 explores the range of contexts and conditions that brought about the settlement of the Cape Verdean Islands in the first place, and then notes the forces that brought Cape Verdeans to New England. Here I attempted to explain the relationship between the economy of the New England coastline and that of the west coast of Africa. I also tried to address the rise of global economic relations accompanying these migrations and the sociopolitical and cultural division of labor imbedded therein. I further document in this chapter how it came to pass that Cape Verdeans established a community in Fox Point.

Chapter 3 addresses questions related to the cultural division of labor that emerged in Providence as Cape Verdeans settled the waterfront area called Fox Point. Were there specific economic activities that brought them there? Was the culture they produced in Fox Point a phenomenon related to their history or a condition that emerged from the development of American society and economy? Were they passive in relationship to the economic forces that oppressed them as an immigrant group, as members of the poor working class, and as a racial minority? Chapter 4 continues this line of questioning, but focuses on the struggle against racism and exploitation. The use of verbatim accounts provides greater depth to the quality of the Cape Verdean longshoreman experience and illustrates the poetic nature of the older generation.

Chapter 5 reflects on the consolidation of the Cape Verdean ethnic community and the homogenization of the culture. Questions centered on the struggle against racism are addressed in this context. For example, were Cape Verdeans able to reproduce their ethnic identity, while also developing a Black identity? Chapter 6 presents the discourse of planners in the context of urban renewal policies which served to sever Cape Verdeans from their neighborhood. What was the rationale for displacing the people of Fox Point? Chapter 7 focuses on Manny Almeida's Ringside Lounge as one point of resistance and unity. It is here that the question of why Manny Almeida's Ringside Lounge became a Cape Verdean bar is answered. Chapter 8 is the last chapter. It summarizes my findings and provides closure in regard to the Fox Point Cape Verdean experience.

Chapter 2

The Beginning

In 1975, the Cape Verdean Islanders liberated themselves from obsolete Portuguese colonialism after a colonial history of five hundred years. Settled in 1460 by the Portuguese and by African slaves, the Cape Verde Islands have evolved into a "melting pot" of cultures and identities. By the end of the sixteenth century, Portugal's control had expanded into the Atlantic and along the West African coastline. Madeira was already mapped in the fifteenth century by the Portuguese, who were first there in 1402. The Azores were settled in the 1430s, the coast of Mauritania was reached in 1445, and the islands of São Tomé and Príncipe in the Gulf of Guinea in 1470. Settlement of the Cape Verdean Islands coincided with the emergence and early expansion of capitalism in Europe.

At first, African gold and spices attracted European traders, who bartered textiles, brass utensils, glass beads, and later Brazilian tobacco in exchange. Only later did Portuguese commerce in West Africa become dominated by the global slave trade. Still, even from the beginning slaves were among the most lucrative trade items. This mixing of peoples and cultures through trade and subjugation was part of the colonial experience. As slavery became a predominantly European commercial venture, Europeans were able to press their advantages and came to dominate a global economic system where the distinctions of skin color and racial or family history became increasingly significant characteristics of identity.

The global division of labor by skin color became increasingly pronounced with the centrality of agriculture in the development of capitalism and its expansion into the Americas. Intensive agriculture on the Cape Verdean Islands, a product of the world's first plantation experiments, was subject to fluctuations of Africa's Sahelian desert climate. Rapid deforestation and soil erosion, caused by periodic and long-term droughts, brought on further environmental deterioration in addition to cycles of impoverishment. A variety of agricultural systems evolved on the various islands, depending on climate and terrain, including small-scale animal husbandry, subsistence horticulture, and small plantation farming. Each of the ten populated islands had natural limitations and economic possibilities whose conditions helped create their specific historical developments. For example, São Tiago is the largest of the Cape Verdean Islands and part of the leeward constellation of islands. While rocky and mountainous, this island has constant fresh water sources that allowed for the growth of towns and cities, of which Praia, the present capital city of Cape Verde, is most prominent. São Tiago, so close to the West African mainland, became a critical center of the slave trade. Its economic importance brought on a political struggle between local-level and crown control over the island that colored much of its early history. Moreover, European interests in dominating the slave economy caused the French, English, and Dutch to fight the Portuguese on this island, where most of the population was made up of African slaves who raised livestock and other commodities supporting international trade and where large quantities of fresh water could be found. Brava, the smallest of the leeward island group, also had water that flowed from its mountainous terrain and that watered the many fertile valleys of the island. Further settlement took place from the neighboring island of Fogo, where a volcanic eruption in 1680 displaced a large number of descendents of the slave population that had started to work Fogo's crown lands in the 1460s. Brava's safe harbors and water attracted shipping, and its small size in relation to its relatively large population helped bring about the migration to New England, where Cape Verdeans were known as Bravas. Boa Vista, Fogo, Maio, Sal, Santa Luzia, Santo Antão, São Nicolau, and São Vicente make up the other islands of this archipelago, each with its own characteristics and developmental history. What is of interest to us here is that the settlement of the islands was socioculturally heterogeneous, displaying a pattern of racial and cultural distinctions which today people still identify through skin color and shades that they trace to either African or Portuguese origins, points of reference that have become powerful features of ethnic identity among Cape Verdeans of New England.

The settling of Providence was different from that of the Cape Verde Islands, although the conditions under which colonization occurred were similar. Capitalism had likewise penetrated the economies of North American indigenous societies, which were united through colonialism with disparate parts of the world into zones of production for one global economy. In New England, of course, it was the British rather than the Portuguese who launched the colonial enterprise, but the same mercantile spirit and quest for large profits—in this case, in fur and ship's timbers— drove them on.

By 1700, Providence's population had grown to 1200 people. While agriculture sustained the town, proximity to the open sea made commerce more lucrative. The profits gained from the Rhode Island merchant trade of rum and slaves built up Providence as much as any coastline New England town. New England was developed by its participation in the West Indies trade, importing molasses and exporting lumber, fish, and other foodstuff and raw materials. However, Providence, more than other New England centers of commerce, was financially dominated by trading in slaves. Slaving was speculative, with merchants risking bankruptcy, but offered the potential of great profits. Some traders earned as much as 300 per cent on their investments while others lost all.

Alcohol and slave trading initiated the contact between the settlers of Providence and the Cape Verde Islanders and inexorably bound these two areas of the world, once separated both by the Atlantic and by their distinctive ways of life. Through trade, Europeans introduced their potent alcoholic beverages to indigenous people all over the world and, when employing these people, included alcohol as part of their wages. The conditions that brought slavery into being made humans into objects of labor for sugar production, distilling alcohol in large quantities, and for trade.

The merchants of Providence directly involved themselves in the European trade of slaves, alcohol, furs, weapons, and other luxuries as the British colonies were brought into intimate economic association, consuming each others' products. Providence quickly assumed its role in this global economy as its population grew and prospered. Although agriculture was the primary means of existence, it was commerce that made possible the amassing of great wealth.

As early as 1680, Elder Pardon Tillinghast of Providence received the right to build a storehouse and wharf, the first in the town, located north of Transit Street. Here, in the area now known as the East Side, Fox Point, and College Hill, the settlement of Providence came into being and grew. Like other Providence merchants, Tillinghast was involved in trade with the West Indies and Africa. Rhode Island farm and dairy products, dried fish, beef, pork, and lumber were transported on Yankee vessels that returned with molasses, sugar, and cotton. African slaves were brought to the West Indies to work on sugar plantations and to the South to work on cotton plantations. The Atlantic trade has sometimes been called the "triangular trade," evoking a simplistic image of goods movement between Africa, the West Indies, and the United States. In actuality, trading relationships were much more complicated and movements of goods took many directions.

What is clear, however, is that alcohol was an important item of trade, as both a commodity and a drug. Some merchants used alcohol to increase sales or to barter for other goods. A Bristol, Rhode Island shipowner, for example, instructed his captain in a manner that was replicated in dealings with indigenous people all over the world. Simeon Potter wrote, "Make yr. Cheaf Trade with the Blacks and Little or more with the white people if possible to be avoided."(Potter's strategy was based on the belief that Africans were easier to cheat than Europeans.) "Worther yr. Rum as much as possibe," Potter continued, "and sell as much by the short mesurer as you can. Order them in the Bots standing ye Son" (Mannix and Cowley 1978:146). By 1770, so many Rhode Islanders were involved in this trade that Samuel Hopkins, pastor of the First Congregational Church in Newport, remarked, "Rhode Island enslaved more Africans than any colony in New England" (ibid).

In 1770, New England rum to Africa accounted for four-fifths of colonial exports. It was used as an item of trade and to help strike favorable bargains. According to Williams, "The Negro dealers were plied with it, were induced to drink till they lost their reason, and then a bargain was struck" (1966:79-80). Profits were reinvested in industry whose growth in Providence was marked by the development of shipbuilding, brick manufacturing, weaving, and distilling in the early eighteenth century, followed by iron works, cider mills, cheese presses, and print shops in the middle of the century, and the start of cotton spinning and jewelry manufacture later on.

The eastern section of Providence continued to grow, and from this central hub, development spread fan-like in a westward and southward direction. The waterfront areas became sites for wharfs, shops, and industries. Early settlers, such as the Power, Tillinghast, and Brown families, all figured conspicuously in the town's affairs and all were involved in the profitable seafaring trade with Africa and the West Indies.

The American Revolution slowed down sea trade and ended the economic supremacy of such towns as Newport, Rhode Island, where people had become dependent on this specialized economic activity. Economic prosperity in Providence, in contrast, evolved from more profitable commercial ventures which stimulated internal markets. The city emerged from the revolutionary conflict as the most viable economic settlement in the region. Providence investors continued to support sea trade after the Revolution, undertakings that helped finance American industrial development. In 1781 alone, 129 sailing vessels docked in Providence, and in 1800, fifty-eight wharfs could be counted along the city's waterfront (College Hill 1967:26).

At the urging of waterfront property owners, Providence town leaders defined the shipping channels in 1815 and established the pattern of docks and shops on the west side of the river. Those who could commissioned houses in the Georgian style, building them some distance from the riverfront. In 1817, a waterfront highway was laid down along Water Street, parallel to the west harbor line from Market Square to Fox Point. With foresight, council leaders and landowners agreed that the land between the new highway and the river would remain open. In the middle of the nineteenth century, a court decision set aside this provision and gave developers a green light for the erection of what architectural historian John Hutchins Cadey described as an "ill assortment of unattractive waterfront buildings, mostly of wood construction, between Crawford Street and Fox Point" (Cadey 1957:83).

Those who had made money in the sea trade invested in new manufacturing concerns. In 1790, in nearby Pawtucket, America's first cotton mill was founded through the skill and entrepreneurial prowess of Samuel Slater and Moses Brown. One year later, Moses joined his brother, John, to open Providence's first bank. While alcohol production and sales remained important for accumulating investment capital, it was the formation of modern industry and financial institutions that brought about a shift in the global economy by further stimulating the need in the United States for poorly paid wage labor.

As whale and seal hunting for mammal oils increased, profits

27

SAM BECK

decreased in the trade of alcohol, and decades-old laws against docking slave ships in Rhode Island ports began to be effectively enforced. Advances in technology and production methods in the region's textile industry made New England the leader in America's industrial economy. Capital once devoted to slaving and merchant shipping was invested in spinning and weaving mills. Agriculturalists and artisans became industrial workers. With industrialization, the need for labor exploded into a stream of movement to America by people from all over the world.

This growth in the former colonies was accompanied by declining fortunes elsewhere, as in Cape Verde, where repeated droughts and periods of famine forced the islanders to seek employment abroad. From one generation to the next, land had been broken up among heirs so that many people held only small parcels. Men without land or with small holdings were encouraged to leave for employment elsewhere, while women remained behind. This movement of people helped ease, at least for a moment, the population pressure on the land, not only through the reduction in population size, but also through the availability of income supplements sent home by migrant workers.

Yankee shippers preferred Cape Verdean seamen because they had a reputation for working hard, accepting low wages, and working as a disciplined crew. It remains difficult to determine what sort of Cape Verdean individuals joined the whaling fleets that plied the oceans, but according to Almeida et al., "usually the young men who shipped out were of the lower classes (and) darker skinned. . . . Many times they returned as poor as they left" (1978:20).

For some, whaling was not the best solution to adverse conditions on the islands. It was a perilous occupation. An eighty- or ninety-foot whale could easily make kindling of an entire boat, killing the crew in the process. Accidents often occurred aboard whaling ships; bones were broken and flesh pierced, and bad food and water brought on slow death. When the dangers of the voyage and hunt were overcome, other perils lurked. Monotony caused harm to crews when whales were not spotted or during periods of calm. Mutinies occurred and fear of desertion forced many a captain to stay at sea for longer periods of time. Despite such miserable conditions, by the early nineteenth century, almost 40 percent of Nantucket's whaling crews were Cape Verdeans (ibid:18).

As empires competed for access to natural resources, contact between disparate parts of the world was intensified. Europeans came to dominate non-Western societies and controlled local economic production. Their large-scale experiments in plantation farming, whaling, and

28

factories required enormous amounts of labor. The "excess" of agrarian labor on the islands pushed many Cape Verdeans to find other means of making a living. Responding to the limitations of their lands and to the brighter economic opportunities available elsewhere, many Cape Verdeans settled in New England, where whaling vessels docked and where the emigrating "Portuguese" remained and clustered to form neighborhoods. By the early nineteenth century, New Bedford, Massachusetts, which had replaced Nantucket as New England's most active whaling port, also became a magnet for Cape Verdean settlements.

As waterpower was replaced by steam, the demand for labor increased. Demand for coal and cotton stimulated the further development of Providence and neighboring ports. Although whaling declined, dock work increased, since the wharf established in colonial times continued to play an important role in waterfront commerce in Providence and elsewhere. Who exactly was involved in the loading and unloading of ships in those days remains unclear. However, it is safe to say that as the Irish, Southern and Eastern Europeans, and others arrived, from the middle of the nineteenth century on, the least skilled, the most recent arrivals, and others who were for various reasons willing to take on the lowest paying work ended up on the docks. Such was the fate of many Cape Verdeans.

Dock work was always episodic, since it depended on the arrival or departure of goods. While many immigrants shuddered at the insecurity of dock work, they had no other choice but to seek employment on the wharfs. Cape Verdeans were accustomed to irregular work, whether at sea, on docks, or in the shipping trades. They worked as riggers, longshoremen, and coopers, and are reported to have played a significant role in the rope works at New Bedford.

Cape Verdeans chose their habitations on the perimeters of working poor neighborhoods. Often, they settled where other people of color were located—Indians, descendents of New England slaves, and free Blacks—and near working poor Southern and Eastern Europeans. It is uncertain if Cape Verdeans settled in Providence's Fox Point before 1862, the year that the Emancipation Proclamation was signed, legally restoring freedom to most American slaves. What is certain is that Cape Verdeans settled with their own identity, one that separated them from association with Afro-Americans or Indians.

Cape Verdeans were doubly stigmatized for being black and for their association with Portuguese language and culture. Yet their color made them more like Black Americans than their Portuguese cultural affilia-

SAM BECK

tion made them like "white ethnics." In America, despite self-denial and
denial of their chosen identity by others, discrimination based on color
gave definition to Cape Verdean identity, neighborhoods, work opportunities, and lifestyles. Furthermore, while white Americans
discriminated against Cape Verdeans as Black people, Black Americans
questioned the Cape Verdean sense of being different. Cape Verdeans
could claim European (Portuguese) descent and voluntary migration,
which they expressed as "having family." "Having family" dissociated
them from early Black American history and unified them as a group
through their vast kin networks (more about this below).

Local tradition held that the Irish moved into Fox Point in the nineteenth century and were quickly joined by the "Portuguese" of the
Atlantic Islands. In retrospect, Cape Verdeans saw themselves as among
the first to make up the Fox Point neighborhood and only in part as
replacing the Irish. In the 1980s, Cape Verdeans claimed Fox Point as
"our neighborhood," in a selective account of Providence's settlement
history. The desire to regain a sense of community based on shared ter-
ritory helped Fox Point Cape Verdeans to repulse deculturation while
simultaneously allowing acculturation in American society to take place.

Cape Verdeans came to New England to better their life standing and
this they accomplished. Opportunities were far greater in America than in
the homeland, which for many was defined by poverty and hunger. For
example, despite relief efforts during the particularly severe drought
years of 1856 and 1857, one-fourth of the Cape Verdean population died
of famine, cholera, and smallpox epidemics. Such conditions compelled
Cape Verdeans to leave their islands, men having access to shipping
trades. Under these conditions, some port women were pressed to offer
their bodies in exchange for food and drink. Although working for low
wages was indisputably better than starving, the conditions under which
Cape Verdeans had to live in both their island homelands and America
were deeply influenced by their skin color and their place within the world
economic system.

However, not all Cape Verdeans were poor. Their emigration pattern to the United States was in keeping with that of other groups. It was
often the middle peasantry of Europe that could afford the expense of
traveling to America, while the poor and destitute remained behind as
cheap labor in the homeland. Not unlike their European counterparts,
some Cape Verdeans were able to take their difficult place in the global
division of labor and profit from it; most could not. Some whalers, for
instance, were able to save their earnings and wisely invested them in
profitable ventures. By the turn of the century a few were able to pur-

chase old whaling vessels that appeared on the market as mammal oil ceased to be profitable and steamships became a more popular means of transportation.

Cape Verdean sea captains sailed their ships between American and African ports. This was called the "packet trade," and carried cargo, mail, and passengers among Cape Verdean settlements dispersed from the homeland. For decades, into the middle of the twentieth century, the packet trade was a fundamental part of Cape Verdean existence and identity. People on shore waited for the ships to arrive with news from friends and relatives, and when the ships arrived crowds gathered. Every family saved to fill barrels with clothing and other goods to send back to the Islands to help relatives at home. Some who invested in this trade became wealthy and obtained the respect of their countrymen in New England and in the Islands.

Passengers came to America to work and traveled the packets when returning home for a visit or to stay. For decades the pattern remained of men going to work abroad, while women remained on the Islands. Not until settlements were established and sedentary lives were possible did women arrive and take their place in creating Cape Verdean communities in New England. The cause of this change in women's status lay in new work conditions.

Besides the dock and shipping crew work, dominated by men, new job opportunities opened in the textile mills and the cranberry bogs. Seasonal berry picking was work in which Cape Verdeans were said to excel (Halter 1984). Entire families participated, living in the sheds provided them until the picking season ended. According to some, the packet trade carried seasonal workers to New England, arriving in the summer and returning in the fall (Almeida et al. 1978:30). People exchanged places with relatives or friends, using the United States passport of one individual to enter, while the original passport holder sailed to Cape Verde for a visit. Some packet trade schooners arrived with stowaways. Secret departures from the Islands were common for those who sought to avoid induction into the Portuguese army and who could not pay for their passage across. Cape Verdeans desiring to come to America, it appears, found the means for doing so. Seasonal work—though requiring trans-Atlantic voyages—provided economic opportunities while allowing for the maintenance of ties with the homeland.

The new U.S. immigration law of 1917 was intended to restrict immigrant arrivals by requiring literacy, but was not enforced strictly enough to hamper the continued flow of Cape Verdeans to this country.

The 1921 restrictions were even more stringent; quotas were applied to severely limit new immigrants and visitation. Cape Verdeans feared being denied reentry to the United States because many were unsure about their status as citizens and thus did not travel home. Resistance to these laws, though, grew as the influx of illegal entries continued (ibid:32-35). The packet trade was crucial to Cape Verdean existence, linking the Islands and the United States even during the Second World War. The last packet ship crossing of the Atlantic took place in 1970 (ibid:42).

By the time the packet trade came to be operated by Cape Verdeans, the islanders had established vigorous communities on Cape Cod, Nantucket, Dorchester, New Bedford, and Fall River in Massachusetts and in Providence and East Providence in Rhode Island. Initial Cape Verdean settlement of the Fox Point area in Providence might have occurred as early as the eighteenth century. Possibly, Cape Verdeans came here during the period of slavery and rum trading, when trading vessels were resupplied in Cape Verde and islanders might have joined sailing crews. However, it is more likely that when whaling and dock work were economically vigorous in Providence in the nineteenth and twentieth centuries, Cape Verdeans moved from New Bedford and Nantucket to Cape Cod and Fox Point. They moved into the poor area that was predominantly Irish, although Portuguese Azoreans had also moved in, and commerce in the neighborhood was dominated by Jews, Syrians, and Chinese.

Cape Verdean contact with, and eventual settlement in, New England coincided with three periods of economic development. Initially, Yankee slavers and rum traders carried Cape Verdean crews, picked up en route to and from the west coast of Africa. As the slavery and rum trades came to an end, Yankee commercial ventures turned to whaling and Cape Verdean whalers became important sources of labor. During the second period whalers remained in American ports for only short periods, on their return voyages. But as whaling intensified, Cape Verdeans remained in port longer and as this industry slowed, on-shore employment became possible. Cape Verdeans in this period were called "Bravas," after the name of one of the islands from which they predominantly came. These men were lighter in skin color than the populations of the other islands, a result, it is thought, of the proximity of Brava Island to the sea lanes, which resulted in increased sexual unions between European mariners and Afro-Portuguese settlers of that island. With permanent land-based employment possible, women and family members joined their men, and active Cape Verdean community life began in New England. The third period occurred with the Cape Verdean-run packet trade. At this time, new opportunities had opened and a new type of immigrant arrived. Instead of the lighter-colored Brava islanders, the darker people from the other islands traveled to America (Machado 1978:54). Yet another period of migration came about after 1975, when the construction of socialism on the islands started and new US immigration laws permitted additional Cape Verdeans to settle in New England. Thousands of these new migrants came to reside in Pawtucket, next to Providence, where they established a sense of community that is different from, although building upon, the one that was created by the initial Cape Verdean settlements in New England.

Chapter 3

South Main Culture

By 1857, Providence had spread in all directions, with a growing population of 50,000 people, yet vacant lots made up much of College Hill. Canal Street, South Water Street, and India Point became centers for iron foundries, a print works, a screw company, a bleachery, and an engine works. Mill owners, industrialists, and merchants were accordingly inspired to move and build their homes on the southern end of Benefit and along Prospect Streets, giving them a fine view of the city and also removing them from industrial commotion and dirt. The settlement also stretched along Angell and Hope Streets and further east on Cooke and Governor Streets. Main Street was primarily residential, with mansions lining the street. These were converted into shops or demolished to make way for new businesses, and those who could afford to moved up the hill into new residential areas. The architecture reflected changes in style as the red brick and clapboard Georgian and Federal structures of the past were replaced by Greek Revival and Italianate structures. Such buildings, high and heavy in scale, with bracketed cornices and Italian classical porticoes, are still to be seen in Fox Point, legacies of the Civil War period.

By the end of the nineteenth century, what today is known as the East Side had taken shape. Those who could afford to had abandoned the waterfront, leaving behind the poor and new immigrants who were continually arriving in Providence. By the close of the nineteenth century, exclusive schools and residential areas had become concentrated on the East Side, which came to represent the seat of power of the political and economic elite of the city. From the hill, the elite looked down and oversaw the development of the city.

This division of residential and economic development increasingly distinguished Fox Point from the East Side. The development of two identifiably separate yet complementary neighborhoods helped crystallize class, religious, ethnic, occupational, and racial distinctions. The enclosure of Fox Point gave rise to a working-class-based behavior among the people living there, creating a new sense of mutual identity and interdependency uncharacteristic of the waterfront's more heterogeneous populations of the previous era. While the establishment of ethnic communities in the United States was common, as new immigrants strove to quickly adapt to changing conditions, an adequate understanding of the emergence of Fox Point as a Cape Verdean community is possible only within the context of local political-economic processes. Although Cape Verdeans settled in neighborhoods in close proximity to each other, they also developed a patchwork quilt of cultural enclaves that to this day punctuate the urban landscape. Cape Verdean men's place in the local labor market, dominating the longshoreman trade, contributed further to their ethnic identity.

Continued Cape Verdean immigration and settlement in Fox Point brought people together from the different islands. By the time Cape Verdeans came to Providence in significant numbers, they had settled into what was one of the oldest and most deteriorated parts of the city. Despite relatively poor living conditions and dubious employment possibilities, Cape Verdeans made their homes along South Main and adjoining streets until the early 1960s Fox Point residents, whether related or not, referred to each other as "family."

South Main Street came to represent a social unity that was special to Fox Point Cape Verdeans, one that set them apart from other ethnic neighborhoods in the area. They were clearly different from the Azoreans (or "White Portuguese") living in Fox Point and from the residents of Providence Italian neighborhoods. Cape Verdeans spoke about Fox Point in a special manner. "Here people could depend on each other," Fox Pointers would say; resources were shared and children were at home in everyone's kitchen. Street life played a central role in people's social lives; the riverfront work place, the neighborhood street scene, and the home were all intimately tied together. Cape Verdeans savored their kin ties; everyone was part of everybody else's life, and it was this conjuncture of qualities that served to produce "South Main culture."

Few knowledgeable observers of the evolving Providence scene deny that the areas settled by Cape Verdeans in Fox Point lacked resources for maintenance of properties, nor that landlords neglected their obligations toward their tenants. People talked about Fox Point as being "rundown and poor." It was described by one fifty-year-old Fox Pointer as having been "the original slum in Providence." Still, it was home to the Cape Verdeans. And for most ot them, it was more than home, it was a way of life. From the turn of the century until the close of "urban renewal" in the 1960s, South Main Street was the center for Providence Cape Verdeans, and today when South Main is mentioned in the company of displaced residents, the response is one of inevitable nostalgia. South Main is lovingly remembered as a place—even a time of life—that was "wonderful," despite the difficulties and material deprivations. The three generations that lived there created and now remain the memory banks of South Main culture. Fox Point Cape Verdeans identified with the street of their childhood and, for some, their parents' memories of the neighborhood. Particular street names evoked a sense of belonging among Fox Point Cape Verdeans that other street names could not. For Cape Verdeans, South Main Street was the essence of Fox Point. It was here and along nearby side streets that they lived. "South Main Street" became a shorthand way of referring to the Cape Verdean neighborhood and way of life in Providence. An administrator of the local VISTA program, a Cape Verdean in his early forties, revealed that to him and his friends, their neighborhood was "Fox Point, and Fox Point was South Main Street. Fox Point was Brook Street. It wasn't Transit Street. It wasn't Wickenden Street. For the most part, it was South Main Street to the corner of Benefit and Wickenden and this is where we were; where we tended to hang out as kids" (CETA Video 1979).

Those who lived in Fox Point shared other experiences that further distinguished them from the other ethnic groups in the city. As an example, the VISTA administrator recalled, "My mother and father had this thing; when they spoke Crioulo, you answered in Crioulo. There was no foolishness. There was none of this . . . kind of American independence in the home. There is none of that stuff. You were told to do things, and you in fact did them. You were given a great sense of . . . pride of what you were . . . in that when you were faced with a situation, you went out and you solved the problem. You did solve the problem! That is not to say that you didn't have help from other people, but basically you initiated whatever you wanted to get done. For example, a lot of us who were born on South Main Street were absolutely poor. By that I mean absolute versus relative poverty . . . there was nothing to compare our poverty against because we were all poor on South Main Street. When I was fifteen years old, I decided, 'Well, OK I need some money.' I had to make some money. OK I was like a teenage kid. Well what did I want money for? What do you want money for? To buy clothes. What else? To impress girls and all this business. OK fine. Well, I went to work on the waterfront. Why? That was the logical thing for Cape Verdean kids, or Cape Verdean American kids, to do. Number one, you could walk from your house to the docks, basically. You knew people that worked there. You knew that they would help you out on the docks. And you made good money. I was fifteen years old and I was making almost three dollars an hour. As a kid! OK! Those are the kinds of things that were taught you. I don't mean that my mother or my father said that this is what you should be; that you should have pride in who you are and pride in whatever you do. They didn't say those things. Because I am not sure they knew how to say them" (ibid).

People of this man's generation and that of his parents also mentioned that the common poverty that affected everyone in Fox Point unified them, whether Black or white, Portuguese, Jewish, Irish, or Syrian. Such unity, at least from the contemporary Cape Verdean perspective, was so strong that a common "Fox Point" identity overruled and made irrelevant the issue of race (color) or ethnicity (specific cultural, linguistic, and historical identities). Such a capacity for incorporating individuals into quasi-kin relationships, despite significant differences, made the Fox Point Cape Verdean identity particularly vigorous, distinguishing it from the more exclusionary ethnic enclaves in the areas around them. I commonly heard from men from thirty-five to seventy-five that they had not felt discrimination. As one man in his fifties notes, "I didn't know I was Black until I left Fox Point." Color was not an issue within the community and did not become one until people left or the community was penetrated by outsiders with different values and priorities which they would struggle to maintain.

Socializing took place on the waterfront, in homes, and on South Main Street, where people made necessary connections with family and friends to get jobs for themselves and for others. The street and the various shops, stores, restaurants, taverns, and similar establishments were public places where men and sometimes women and children would hang out. Most everything required by a household was available in the neighborhood, restricting the need to venture outside. For those who did work outside, or in settings where contact with outsiders occurred, such interaction was placed into another frame of reference that separated the neighborhood reality from non-neighborhood contexts.

Although this sort of socializing was important in earlier periods and even in the islands of Cape Verde, it cannot be attributed only to the maintenance of traditions. This sort of behavior was a response to real conditions which existed in Fox Point as they did on the Islands: a lack of resources, combined with possibilities of obtaining them, motivated people to support each other in the hope that benefits obtained by one would be redistributed to others. Such redistribution did occur as Cape Verdean migrants sent back home tons of clothing and food along with tools, sewing machines, agricultural implements, and other artifacts of American technology.

While people felt no or little discrimination within Fox Point, discrimination against Black people was a fact of life, drawing people together as a response. Immigration laws had restricted and virtually cut off travel from the homeland. Such separation presumably caused people to depend on each other even more, bringing about a consolidation and homogenization of a distinctly Fox Point Cape Verdean culture. Such matters as poverty, street life, and even Prohibition and illicit alcohol production, tightened family and community relations. Economic deprivation solidified codes of community assistance and led to cooperation even when resources were scarce. Getting jobs did depend more on who you knew than qualifications to do the work (although these helped). The political and economic conditions of developing capitalism on a global scale brought about internationalization of labor, production, and consumption. Ethnic enclaves that became defined as communities and neighborhoods were both a response or adaptation to conditions of immigration and a resistance to those forces responsible for further separating people from those social and cultural roots that emphasized kinship relations and cooperation.

Longshoreman work depended on personal networks since the work was periodic and seasonal and knowledge of available work was a matter of "knowing people who knew." An individual had to act fast when news of arriving ships spread into the neighborhood because many people competed for membership on work crews. Everyone was tied to everyone else and so the competitive advantage was subtle. As a member of a work crew, a man had to be dependable and "true to his word." By performing poorly on the job, one man could jeopardise the performance and reputation of the entire crew and hence impact directly on the livelihood of his family, friends, and neighbors. In the period between the two world wars and into the early 1950s, Cape Verdean men were primarily involved in occupations in which being well-connected and dependable as members of work crews determined job opportunities. They worked as longshoremen, in construction trades, and as coalboat laborers. Many had seamen's cards, too, according to one longshoreman, "because if things were slow on the docks, you could always ship out."

These were not the only jobs in which people were engaged. In the summer, recalled one middle-aged man, "me and the family picked cranberries from Labor Day until the first of October. In the summer we picked strawberries for about thirty days (June and July) and then we picked blueberries. We used to live in shacks for free, getting paid piece work at two cents a box. We went down with our own money to pay for the food we bought and prepared it ourselves. The people stayed on for each crop. There was little social life; no parties, only the old timers played cards. People used to go to places like Carver and Wareham, Massachusetts as seasonal workers." The same person continued, "All Cape Verdean sections (people from different neighborhoods in New England) used to combine from all over, working in the fields. It was a Cape Verdean project." The labor force for these crops, according to Cape Verdeans, was exclusively Cape Verdean (see Halter 1984 for greater detail). "The white people owned it (the crops and the fields). We were poor, but we managed," one man told me. Seasonal agricultural labor was a family affair: young and old, men and women participated as best they could to contribute to the household.

In the 1980s, men had a tendency to remember their mothers as having stayed at home, despite their awareness that a number of mothers had held jobs as domestics who washed and cleaned and cooked for the wealthier people of Providence. Members of the community recalled that these domestic workers primarily worked for the people of the East Side. One forty-seven-year-old Cape Verdean said that such women in particular "could go to work and come back before the kids returned from school." This made it seem as if mothers were home all of the time. "I didn't find out about this," he said, " until just a few years ago, when my mother's best friend died and people spoke of her as a domestic with a reputation as one of the best. I didn't know that! I thought she stayed home all day, like my mother!" Women also continued to work in New

England textile mills, and, according to two middle-aged men, were instrumental in finding jobs for their children. One man told of how they and another friend worked at the "Esmond Mill." Speaking of their first jobs, he recalled "My mother took me to work in a factory working from three to eleven making cotton—baling and stacking. We worked in the picking room. The railroad," he said of his second job, "was a better job; it was better money."

When asked why he switched work, he pointed at his friend sitting at the counter of Dave's Grill, where we were having our conversation, and said with a smile, "He got us fired . . . and we left together." Defending himself from this slight on his character, the man at the counter responded that they had been fired together, because both had been working two jobs and were caught sleeping on the night shift in the cotton factory. He explained that they had been working as day laborers on the coal boats at the same time and were very tired.

"Working on the railroad was not only hard—we worked like a bastard!—but it was dangerous, too," recalled the first man. They worked on tampering gangs, raising tracks and resetting them. "We worked under age," he said. They were about fourteen years old or so. From the railroad they moved on to become longshoremen because "one of our friends got killed on the railroad job." The two men told the story together, as each filled in the pauses and lapses in the other's memory. Their friend was hit by a train and died. "So we decided to leave the railroad! . . . He hung with us, he was our friend. We saw him get killed. He was walking up the tracks. The compressors made a lot of noise—he didn't hear the train. He," (the friend sitting at the counter) "yelled to warn the friend, but he didn't hear." From the restaurant counter, a choked-up voice yelled, "I ran toward him, but he was turned away from me and didn't see me." The man who began the story pointed to his old friend and said, "He saw it all. After that we all scattered. That was around forty-eight or forty-nine."

This man got married in 1950 and by 1953 left the waterfront to work on a steady job at the Narragansett Parking Garage, opposite the Narragansett Hotel. Because the boats were slow and he had a baby to support, he could not afford to wait for dock work to reappear. According to him, his wife also pressured him to look for something steady. In 1966, the shipping trade had once again developed momentum "as a result of the Vietnam War," he said, and he went back to more lucrative waterfront work. Concerning his movement in and out of jobs, he explained that "any move was an improvement." He said that when he did not work on boats he was able to collect workmen's compensation (he probably meant unemployment insurance) and hung out along South Main.

The people around him fondly remembered those good old days on South Main. With everyone in agreement, he continued, "We were a happy lot. . . . Maybe the new generation has changed; when we were growing up people helped each other out. For example, home fuel in the past was coal and wood. In the summer all the neighborhood would saw wood; everybody helped each other. Four or five men worked, while the women cooked. We used to have a shed for wood and bins for coal. . . . No one knew about locks and keys. That's what we're losing," he reflected, his hand tucked under his chin: "Every generation changes. If you were sick back then, neighbors would come and clean and cook for you."

He stopped talking abruptly, leaving unstated what people in Grill usually came around to talk about, the comparison of the present in terms of ideal, oppositional types. Everyone talk this, even teenagers who never experienced South Main Street versation always came around to the present fear in the neigh' break-ins and thefts and of how "you don't even know your ... And how "people no longer help each other out," contrasted to the when people were "family," and lived in harmony and trust. And how "you didn't have to lock your doors when you left the house."

In talking about the South Main period, one man volunteered that "the second most dangerous industry in the United States is longshoremen's work!" It was precisely this work with which most Cape Verdean men in Fox Point were occupied. It was work, according to some of the old-timers, that white people didn't want to do. It was hard work and dangerous. It was insecure work, with most families experiencing feast or famine. There was money when there was work, and work was available when ships came in. It was a system to which virtually all in Fox Point were subjected, since most families, according to the men, depended on the wages brought by longshoremen.

As with other people of color, the Cape Verdeans found difficulty in participating in the economic and social circle of other immigrants. Being Black in Providence, unskilled and with a poor knowledge of the English language, restricted most Cape Verdeans to work as hod carriers, coal shovelers, and dockworkers. Still, there were exceptions; people educated themselves or gained success in business in their own communities and acquired respect locally and in regional settings.

The importance of kinship to longshoring in Fox Point must not be underestimated. Godparenthood among Cape Verdeans, with its religious and social consequences, became part of getting a job. Godparents sponsored the baptism of their godchildren and under certain conditions acted as co-parents. This means that a *cumpad* (godparent) took on responsibilities for ritual roles and, much like a real parent, was responsible for properly socializing and taking care of the godchild's well-being. The "cumpad" system was reproduced on the docks, as those individuals who were "smart," who could read and write and calculate, became bosses. These men organized work crews for unloading ships and became crucial in the "shaping up" process. They were in effect the "cumpads" of people to whom they were not related by blood or religious ceremony, but for whom they provided favors. This patron-client relationship, too, held the community together.

According to one person, "not everything was a bed of roses. There was tension and conflict, as there is in any family." Before the Second World War, when work was scarce, the competition for work was particularly severe. The "cumpad" could have significant power since he decided who would work. Tensions were part of "cumpad" relationships. Out of the "cumpad" system emerged reliable, fast-working hatch gangs and a subsequent network of social relations that extended into the community. Those men who were not chosen for particular jobs were left to speculate as to the conditions that allowed others to work. Despite the tension that this created, the sense of family, common conditions of poverty, immigrant life, and being Black in a white society sustained Cape Verdeans as a group and unified them. This sense of "family" remained an anchor of identity among Cape Verdeans who matured in Fox Point, one that could be mobilized in times of need.

The "family" in this sense holds a complex set of meanings in which biological links and those established through marriage were foremost in importance, although other members of the neighborhood were not excluded from belonging, Black or white, Cape Verdean or not. This latter sense of family is made up of reciprocating relationships, of obligations and responsibilities inherent in developing social networks. The use of the "family" idiom points to the centrality of kinship, its expression among Fox Point Cape Verdeans, and its significance for developing changing forms of social interaction.

The work and leisure activities of social intercourse were tied together. Because these took place in the same arena they were critical to the development of a distinct Fox Point Cape Verdean identity. The use of the term "family" included people in both work and non-work situations. Those who worked together relaxed together and they were family. When, later on, work and non-work relations were separated, this family sense of neighborhood was replaced by other forms of social interaction. This was for the most part identified by a common sense of history and a periodic sharing of time and activities, such as meetings at Manny Almeida's Ringside Lounge.

When actual kinship was not a factor, friends and work crew members responded to each other as kin might. Repeatedly, Cape Verdeans pointed out that it was the growing up together and experiencing of common conditions of life and work that bound people together and "that" is what was called "family." Cape Verdeans stressed that while they were poor, they shared what they had, even with complete strangers. Carrying this point to an extreme, some people discussing South Main said, " There were bums there, but we Cape Verdeans fed them and took care of them." This form of sharing carried with it a sense of trust and mutual respect, ultimately defined by anticipatory, generalized reciprocity. A favor given could at some point in the future be returned or called for.

It was even more common for youngsters in the neighborhood to be fed wherever they happened to be at meal time, even in homes of non-relatives. Some pointed out that "it was impossible to enter a home without being fed. There was always *canja* (a rice and chicken dish) or *jagacita* (a rice and bean dish) cooking, and to refuse (to eat) was to reject the family connection—by insulting the people." Also common was for children to live with relatives—grandparents, aunts and uncles—and to be raised with the help of friends and neighbors. In those days, "no one was broke, the community was the welfare system. People gave benefit dances. . . . One way or another, they (people needing assistance) got it" (Dicker 1968:18). One old man put it this way: "If I got sick, they helped me out. My brother lost his leg and everyone wanted to buy him a wooden leg. The community fed itself. . . . One hand washed the other." Another frequenter of Dave's Grill remembered that "ship people used to get three to four days off to party up. Often, we'd show a sailor the town, feed 'em, take care of 'em, take 'em back to the boat. A stranger had no problems in Fox Point." On South Main, everyone kept an eye out for everyone else. To Fox Point Cape Verdeans, this was family, community, and neighborhood.

Chapter 4

The Longshoremen's Union

On the basis of kinship, friendship, neighborliness, and shared cultural bonds, seen by outsiders in terms of ethnicity and race, Cape Verdeans wrested a new place for themselves in Providence society and in the local economy and shaped an ethnic identity that was associated with their occupation on the docks. Their place within the economy shifted as the economy itself underwent changes through which workers fought for a place in determining their futures. During the first half of the twentieth century, the economy in Rhode Island suffered a decline affecting, to one degree or another, all workers who were dependent on industrial employment. This economic decline brought pressure on workers to produce more goods for less wages, leading to an increase in labor militancy and the strengthening of the trade union movement. Between 1919 and 1939, employment in the state's textile industry fell 22.1 percent. The rapid decline of the state's textile industry, a decline which was to lead employers in this twenty-year period to ask for a twenty percent wage cut and an increase in the work week to fifty-four hours, resulted in several bitter strikes. During the 1922 strike ethnic boundaries were relaxed, as Portuguese, Greeks, Poles, and other groups banded together and lent support from their respective communities. The primarily Cape Verdean longshoremen were inspired by such local examples of unity among working people.

Many American Blacks, including Cape Verdeans, became increasingly involved in gaining more rights in the laboring process. While limited access to resources defined the lives of Fox Pointers, hemmed into their neighborhood by poverty, skin color, or lack of skills, the politics of union organizing did not pass them by. The political base of the Cape Verdean longshoremen emerged definitively in 1933, when the International Longshoremen's Association Local 1329 qualified for its charter. Non-Cape Verdeans also joined this union in smaller numbers, adding strength to the Longshoremen's local, which was nonetheless organized and led by Cape Verdeans themselves. Earlier attempts to unionize Cape Verdeans had failed. Notable among these was the attempt to bring Cape Verdeans into the Seaman's Union in 1897, when racist sea captains blocked "Negro Portuguese" from joining the union and obtaining the same wage rates as white seamen (Buhle et al. 1983:75) tion of labor by race did not prevent the formation o 1329. I suspect this was the case precisely because the union local was based in ethnicity, that it was primarily organization.

Still, the political base of the Cape Verdean somewhat hampered by the divisions among working people, who were forced to fight each other for jobs and housing. Competition for jobs among an overabundant supply of workers was a central feature of Rhode Island economic development. According to Rhode Island labor historian Paul Buhle, "the merchant kings depended upon the lack of familiarity among workers, language differences and outright ethnic hostilities to forestall a unified resistance." According to Buhle, little has changed. "Many of the same money-aristocracy families which traded in black slavery and white mill worker's misery still exert great influence upon the economy and politics, encourage apathy and corruption . . ."(1983:iii).

While this underlying condition of the poor being governed by the rich has undergone little change in a broad sense, the nature of the distribution and redistribution of wealth has changed as immigrant populations, even people of color, and their descendents have integrated themselves into America's middle-class mainstream. They have had to fight for access to upward mobility through consumerism, occupational specialization, and, despite significant resistance among some Fox Point

Cape Verdeans, movement to new neighborhoods. According to Rhode Island lore, those wishing to enter society must suffer pain, disillusionment, and anguish. One Providence city official told me that "to make the system work, everyone has to pay their dues."

The histories of ethnics and working people in the United States are intertwined. The formation of ethnic and national identities in this country resulted from the competition for jobs and housing among various groups subjected to similar constraints and, as important, possibilities for mobility. In looking for work and places to live, it was the interlocking chain of kin that people sought out for help. Village neighbors or fellow nationals, those sharing a common language or culture, found common understanding and unity. In this manner, people from the different islands of Cape Verde, for example, homogenized their diversity and produced common identities in the context of their new neighborhoods and working conditions.

The period 1884 to 1915 was critical to Rhode Island's ethnic composition. During this period the predominantly "Yankee" population in the state found itself host to successive waves of immigrants. The Irish and French Canadians, already established, were joined by Portuguese and Italians. Industrial development in the area of Providence was the primary incentive attracting immigration. The city's population expanded rapidly. By 1900, Providence was made up of 65,881 American-born and 109,716 foreign-born residents.

TABLE 1

POPULATION GROWTH IN PROVIDENCE

1800	7,614
1820	11,767
1840	23,172
1860	50,666
1880	104,852
1900	175,597

Source: Providence, R.I. City Documents, Volumes 1801-1901.

SAM BECK

Rhode Island politics were dominated by Yankee Republicans whose economic base was rooted in textile mills, associated industries, and finance. They successfully courted some immigrant groups, particularly Italians and French Canadians. Cultural and social clubhouses were set up to handle the immigrant community's problems and ensure their votes. Before 1920, the Democratic Party consisted almost entirely of Irish millhands and laborers and a few Yankee farmers who had little power. While the Republicans were able to amalgamate ethnic support, the Irish-dominated Democrats, according to one student of this issue, were unable to do this because they were too poor to buy the necessary votes (Goering 1968:65).

Despite the massive influx of immigrants, politics remained in the hands of the few because it was not until November 6, 1928 that Article 20 was adopted by the Rhode Island legislature, giving the right to vote to all citizens 21 years of age who had resided in the state for at least two years. Until then, the Bourn Amendment had restricted the vote for city councillors to property holders only. The last distinctions between native-born and naturalized citizens' voting rights were also eliminated in 1928. In 1931 election, the Democratic Party swept through most city councils in the state. By 1932, Theodore Francis Green's efforts to build a Democratic Party from a coalition of ethnic groups, including Cape Verdeans, paid off and as a result he was elected governor that year.

Members of ethnic groups and working people in Rhode Island reached a new phase in their political development, gaining power to ameliorate the oppressive conditions under which they suffered. On November 13, 1933, Local Chapter 1329 of the International Longshoremen's Association received its charter, in no small part due to the efforts of Manuel Q. Ledo, the local labor organizer. He struggled his entire life to create more equitable working conditions for the unskilled, organizing among construction trades, such as the hod carriers, and waterfront trades, such as the coal shovelers and the longshoremen. His organizing prowess was particularly recognized by the longshoremen, who knew Ledo as the "Chief," or the "Rooster." Today, people remember little about him, yet what people do recall provides an important context in which to construct a portrait of Cape Verdean ethnicity, race, and socioeconomic status.

The following oral accounts by four of Manuel Q. Ledo's contemporaries—his daughter and three companions in the labor struggle—not only reveal something of the manner and chronology of his life, but also shed light on his union involvement and the conditions under which the longshoremen operated. These historical recollections can serve as the basis for further work to more fully grasp the significance of the Cape Verdean efforts to acquire political power in the region.

"Tini" Ledo Jackson was in her middle age when I interviewed her and had limited recollections of her father, since she was the youngest of his children. "He came to this country in 1900. His father, Querino Ledo, a seaman aboard one of the whaling ships that brought him here, also brought my father's sister, Mary. They came from the island of Brava and settled in the Harwich-South Dennis area on the Cape. His father had taken another wife in this country, so they went to live there with his new wife. She was a woman named Mary from the Azores. I think they met on the Cape (Cod) . . . I'm not sure. When my grandfather died, she went back to the Azores where she died. They had no children of their own.

"My grandfather's first wife was Guilhermina Gonsalves. The only thing we know about her is from Father's birth certificate, where it says that Manuel Querino Ledo was born on January 16, 1894 in Matino, in the parish of the Nossa Senhora do Monte church. He was the first son to his parents.

"We have no idea why his father brought my father and his sister— took them away from their mother. My father never said. All he ever said was, his father had been aboard the *Morning Star*—I guess out of New Bedford—the whaling ship, and the *Charles W. Morgan*. When I tried to get information about the records, I was told that a lot of the records . . . were destroyed. They couldn't find the name of Ledo in the records of that ship.

"My grandfather was born in 1848 and . . . I don't know how he came about going on whaling ships, but I guess because of poverty those people did do that. My father used to tell us he went all over the world and his father did settle on the Cape—brought him and his sister there to this woman he married.

"His sister Maria went to different schools and got educated. She married a Bermudian who was well off and she died in Bermuda. My father, as far as I learned, only went up to the fourth grade on the Cape. He used to tell us he was embarrassed about going to school. He had to wear his stepmother's shoes.

"My father was real light (in skin color). As a matter of fact he said a story went around that a Russian seaman was his grandfather. You know, this is all so complicated that we don't even know—but my father was lighter than many of the white Portuguese. And my mother said his father was a great big, very light man with red hair. So, we are a kind of mixture. As you know, people of different nationalities went to the Cape Verde Islands—sailors and seamen from all over the world.

"I have very little knowledge of what my father did after he finished school, but I know he shipped out as a very young man. We have a postcard photograph he sent to his sister when she was living in Newport (Rhode Island). I think he sent it in 1913, when he was nineteen years old and on his way from Cuba to Florida.

"I don't know how he got involved in the union, but he did become involved. The CIO, the AF of L—that's all we ever heard growing up. The CIO and AF of L! I don't know much about this, but he had quite a number of friends up on Federal Hill (the politically powerful Italian neighborhood)—the Falco brothers and Judge De Pasquale (all prominent in Democratic politics of the times).

"And then he got involved with the Hod Carriers' Union. He was a business agent for them. These are the men who carry the bricks on their shoulders. When these large buildings were being built in Rhode Island, these were the men who put them up.

"The only other thing I know, in 1933 right after the Depression, my mother came into some money and took us to Florida. My father was left here. When we came back a year later, he had organized the International Longshoremen here in Providence. He was a gay blade. He took care of his men, but paid less attention to his family. My father was the one that put the men where they are today—making good money and working under good conditions."

Willis J. Jones, an African-American octogenarian, worked with Ledo as a coal shoveler and later as a longshoreman. He perceived the racial context of his social surroundings and did not hesitate to point out the racist setting in which he lived. In the process, he quickly divided himself and his fellow Black Americans from the "Portuguese" Cape Verdeans. He said, "Well, you see, before . . . the waterfront when it was Black, it was all Black. My father and them, they were all Black. There weren't any Portuguese . . . only one and that was Paul Mendes.

"At the old Harbor Junction, when they first started shoveling coal down there—that goes way back to nineteen-eight and then afterwards—a lot of Portuguese people came in. And finally, it ended up being all Portuguese (Cape Verdean). All Colored (Black American) were practically all gone but a few.

"The city was segregated to a certain extent then. Of course, in this day and age things have changed from what they were when I was a boy. When I was a boy, certain restaurants, you couldn't go in them. They didn't want you in them. In fact, they wouldn't let you in them. Then they couldn't keep you out. You see, not all the prejudice was in the South; there was a lot of it right here!''

Only three men who worked with Ledo in forming Local 1329 are still living. Among them, ''Toy'' Fernandes and George Diaz are the oldest. Toy was born on the island of Boa Vista in 1908, an only child. He said that ''in 1920, there was a big house there (in New Bedford) where your passport was checked. Your parents and others would be there to receive you when you came from the old country. I came on a three-masted schooner, although most Cape Verdeans used to come on two-masters. We landed in New Bedford. I came seven years after my parents and they followed my Aunt Maria. She really wasn't my aunt; she was a good friend and neighbor on the island and helped us out.

''When I got to Providence, my mother was running a sort of boarding house, paying rent for the floor we lived on. Three or four whaling men roomed there, working at the same time with my father. They would leave their insurance policies in my mother's name—Metropolitan, the only company at the time that used to have collectors come to the door. She would feed the boarders, too. At that time, there wasn't much dock work to do.

''I lived in Fox Point, above the old Union Hall on South Main. But after a month, we moved to East Providence, where my parents bought a house. There weren't too many Cape Verdeans living there then, mostly Italians.

''My father worked on a whaling ship. He could read and write, but my mother could only sign her name. He'd be away five or six months at a time before returning. At that time the ship officers were Norwegians and the crew was all Cape Verdeans.

''When the men were whaling, there wasn't a lot of dockwork in Providence. But when whaling stopped, the dockwork started. Almost all Cape Verdeans came into doing longshoreman work. They knew how to rig the ships, knowing the tonnage of the booms. Ships were carrying a lot of lumber from the West Coast, they were mostly American ships.

''In those days booms were rigged for five tons. If there was more, you took your chances. At that time you didn't have safety. There wasn't the safety check during the unloading process the way you have now. Now with the union, there is a safety man. In those days we had many casualities; people got hurt. You took your chances then. There's been quite a change since the union. Quite a change!

''There is a difference between stevedores and longshoremen. We are the longshoremen who work for the stevedores. John J. Orr" (among the first and few remaining stevedoring companies in Providence) "and the like, for example, are the stevedores. They hire the longshoremen.

"After whaling slowed, my father became a longshoreman and then I became one in 1927. It was hard work. Cape Verdeans were hired because they were people who could be depended on. It was hard work, but it was the only way we could survive. No one else wanted to do it.

"Ships came in with five hatches and each hatch had a gang. Fifteen men to a gang was usual depending on the cargo; more men were used with lumber cargo. One Cape Verdean was a walking foreman; he was the leader. He picked the men and had the capacity to control them. He knew how to write and took your name and turned it into the office for the payroll. He made sure everyone got paid properly. The walking foreman was part of the company and got higher pay on the ship." (This division between those who were salaried by the company and those who were hired on an hourly wage created a division among Fox Point Cape Verdeans that was difficult to overcome.)

"Ledo and I were in the same gang. Ledo used to say to me, 'Toy, we gotta do something different.' We used to work rain and snow. . . . The company used to rob us of our time. We had no control. 'We gotta organize,' he'd say. To organize took some time; we had to sign a petition to become members.

"At that time we had lumber that was coming in from Russia and they hired extra men and Mr. Ledo, as a stickman, was working the piles of lumber with me. Mr. James was the superintendent of the A. C. Dutton Lumberyard in Providence" (a major stevedore concern) "and we were working there. He was very much against the local, which as you know, most of the companies were not in favor of. He told Mr. Ledo and me that we were organizing something that in the future would harm the company. They all wanted for themselves, taking our blood to do it.

"When we were organizing, some of the men didn't want to join. The company put fear into us. Most of our older people were afraid. The company told their walking foremen not to hire Ledo, Fernandes, and so and so. They called us agitators. In 1927, we got paid 50 cents an hour. After 5 o'clock, we got paid 70 cents an hour. Just like slavery they worked us. We worked under all kinds of weather. That's why we decided to organize.

"During this period my father was neutral, as far as the (work) yard was concerned, although we knew he was on our side. I think we really started agitating in 1929. At that time there were only a few of us and there was a one dollar fee to belong. The longer people waited to join, the more it cost.

"Well, anyway, I remember Mr. James; he was a lawyer. He was a smoothy from out of state who came to Providence to make a living off of us. He used to tell us, 'You don't do nothing. . . . You have no schooling!' So, Mr. James had a system, when the ship was through being unloaded, we used to go home. We had no more work. He would have the hatch foreman bring some of the men back the next day to work in the yard. He knew some of the men signed up already; he knew since there were messages going back and forth. Anyway, those who signed up didn't get to work. Mr. James would bring men into work just so they wouldn't sign up!" (The efforts to bring about divisions among the longshoremen took many forms. Yet despite these rifts in status, wages, and political persuasion, everyone recognized that in the final analysis they remained "family.")

"As we went along with the organizing, some of the men got smart and signed. The moment they signed, Mr. James would tell the foreman, 'He doesn't come anymore!' So they got smart. We told them, 'You guys are getting smart now! Mr. James is only using you, using us! He is using the men simply so you won't sign things.' But when we had a majority, all that stopped.

"Mr. Ledo was a great organizing man. But there is another man that shouldn't be forgotten, a man who some of the younger men may not know about. This man we must not forget, that is Mr. John F. Lopes, who was an undertaker (in Fox Point). He always backed and was behind Mr. Ledo because Mr. Ledo, like a longshoreman and good man, before he could settle the business, he used profanity. Mr. Lopes, who went along with him said, 'Here now, we'll take care of this matter much better than that.' And using careful language he did.

"Mr. James could say to him, 'You're not a longshoreman; what are you doing here? You are a businessman.' Mr. James would walk away. Mr. Lopes would tell Mr. James, 'Now wait a minute!' He would turn to Ledo and say, 'You know Ledo, he doesn't want to talk to me; Ledo, call the men from the ships!'

"The moment he did that, Mr. James would say, 'Hold it, hold it! We'll do the business, whatever you want to do.' You see, they respected that man! The truth was that Mr. James did not like blacks.

"Ledo was short and stocky, a light brown man. He was well built, about five feet seven. He would say, 'Men, it's time for us to get together to organize, otherwise we'll just be the way we are now.'

"Now that we're organized, it's different; we have more control over our working conditions. Like anyone else, by organizing we wouldn't be mistreated like we were in that particular time. As you know, once you organize, you're well respected by everyone and also your wages increase. Organizing gave us strength and kept us from being abused. And we were being abused!"

George Dias was two years younger than Toy (seventy-three at the time of the interview) and was born in Fox Point. He remembers well the conditions under which the Cape Verdeans organized the union of longshoremen and as he spoke, his voice at times produced a cadence that can only be described as poetic. He said, "My father worked with rag people, driving a horse and wagon. He got into an accident and hurt his leg, which they amputated, but he died anyway in 1912. My mother was a laundress for forty-five years. She worked for three different people, mostly on the East Side or some wealthy people living off of Benefit.

"When I was five years old I moved to East Providence where there were lots of other Cape Verdeans. In 1912 through 1915, it was like a borough, ten to twelve families were living there. They all bought houses there. Some people farmed. When the war started, we moved back to Fox Point. I spent one year in Jersey City, New Jersey (in 1920 and 1921) where I went to high school. That's when my mother married a second time, a ship steward who died in 1946.

"Eventually, I got back to Fox Point, in 1930, where I've been ever since. I started working on the waterfront on New York boats (that came into Providence). My cousin Marshall Bento brought me down on the ships. It was a Saturday and then money was good and shit . . . forty-two years I've been working as a longshoreman.

"We took ships from Norfolk, Virginia, freight from the South with machinery, box freight, wool, and steel. That was working coastwise; every weekend three ships came out of Norfolk. A steady man would get fifty-five cents an hour; if you weren't part of the gang, you'd get a dime less, forty-five cents. At that time, for $8.00 a month you could rent a mansion. It was hard work! It was a son of a bitch! Walk and talk. Walk and talk. You worked twelve hours a day. Walking fifty miles a day. You had to pick up the lumber. It was all marked. With pig iron, you needed (new) gloves every hour.

"At that time you could bring anyone in. All up and down the dock, it was all strictly 'Black.' " Like Willis Jones, George Diaz addressed the color line in the larger society, but unlike Jones, who made a distinction between Black Americans and "Portuguese" Cape Verdeans, he considered Cape Verdeans Black. Diaz included Cape Verdeans among Blacks to make his point about the nature of exploitation at this time, based on distinctions of color. Culture, ethnic heritage, was not as significant as color. "The only other things you could do," the old man continued, gesticulating with his hand in the air, "if you were a nigger was work in a hotel as a porter or go to the East Side to be a butler or a chauffeur.

"It was hard work, but I was glad to get it. But if it weren't for the union, I'd be a poor cocksucker now! It was hard work; waiting for a boat, waiting, nothing, nothing, nothing! It was transit work. If you went to get a steady job, so you'd get $36.00 a month. The boss was like Jesus Christ! All you needed was a fucking hook and good back! Guys would shine up their hooks with emery cloth to make it gleam. And then they'd put the hook on their shoulders when they were walking around. A hook you could buy for fifty cents at Prester's" (a Jewish storekeeper on South Main Street). "He had canteens for cooked food, saddles, gloves, shoes. . . . It was like an army-navy store today.

"Ledo was my friend. We used to drink together, a regular guy, a big gambler, a good guy. He was called the 'Chief' and the 'Rooster.' Don't ask me why. He was a big man around here. He was a fast talker and was a business agent for the Laborers' Union. In 1928, he pulled a strike at the Industrial National Bank building" (in downtown Providence), "when they were building it. At that time, Ledo was the business agent of the Laborers' Union. Then he came to organize the waterfront in 1933 and became the business agent of the Longshoremen.

"The first and major operation this union struck was in Portsmouth, Rhode Island. Manuel Q. Ledo came on and blew the whistle. He says like, 'We're striking and we want more money!' Then there was Eddie Carroll, boss longshoreman out of Boston. He went like that. He took out a union book and he says, 'Go ahead boys, sign up!' He says, 'I'm a union man out of Boston.' He says, 'Go ahead Manuel, we'll pay the wages . . . seventy-six and one eleven!' Yeah, seventy-six cents and $1.11. That's when it struck in Portsmouth. Not too many men still living who were there. That was the first operation. That was in the spring time and we had 210 guys signed up.

"See, there were a lot of these guys, they wouldn't join that union because that Mr. James was a son of bitch! You know what I mean! If they joined it, they did not want the boss or anybody to know they were coming into the union. You understand what I mean! They were afraid to lose their jobs or something. But when we were chartered, lots of guys came in."

Ultimately, Manuel Q. Ledo was able to integrate the kin-based social system of Cape Verdean immigrants with the political structures that operated to restrict or provide access to resources through formal government mechanisms. The Cape Verdeans in Providence were held together by the bond of "family" in which neighbors and kin helped each other, by low status based on skin color that limited their avenues for social and economic mobility and concentrated them in one neighborhood, and by concentration in one primary occupation (at least for men), longshoring, which helped increase their sense of unity through control of common, known resources. Certainly the opposite tendencies for conflict and disunity were also present, since access to resources for working poor "Black Portuguese" was limited and as a result people seeking work had to compete with each other. Despite the efforts of Mr. James and individuals like him, who tried hard to divide them, the workers "got smart" by unifying under a union charter. James' failure was to the credit of Manuel Q. Ledo, who successfully used his respected place in the Cape Verdean community to negotiate the broader political arenas in which he gained support from Fox Point's wealthy and powerful funeral director Lopes and from the Democratic Party leadership, which wanted to sustain their newly won victory in the state and gain the support of the regional Longshoremen's Association. That it was in eveyone's interest to support the Cape Verdean-led longshoremen's union made it all the better. Irish-dominated Fox Point made a Democratic Party connection critical to Cape Verdean political ventures. It was fortuitous that, according to Fox Pointers, Governor T. F. Green had grown up in Fox Point with the Cape Verdeans. He, like others, was integrated into their "family."

Chapter 5

Fox Point Cape Verdean Identity

As Cape Verdeans discussed the history of their community with me, they identified themselves as "Fox Pointers," distinguishing themselves from the Cape Verdeans living in East Providence and New Bedford. At the time of my research, Cape Verdeans needed to identify themselves to me not only ethnically as Cape Verdeans, but also in terms of their residential community. They were Fox Point Cape Verdeans! What is of particular significance here is that the formation of an ethnic identity included a socially relevant locational identity. The Fox Point Cape Verdean identity was developed in the period of their first arrival in the second half of the nineteenth century, was strengthened and focused in the context of their neighborhood, and then in the 1960s was reaffirmed, but in the context of urban transformation: the combined efforts of historical architectural preservation and urban renewal, displacement, and gentrification.

Until the 1960s, the Cape Verdean community managed to protect itself from the most severe consequences of social deprivation which derived from racial prejudice and low economic status. They created an arena in which positive self-identity grew, and even nourished a second and third generation until they were to suffer the pain of dislocation. The resultant diaspora transformed the Cape Verdeans' neighborhood into an ideology—the neighborhood having disappeared physically while retaining a certain existence in the historical associations of displaced people. The Cape Verdeans dispersed into many parts of the greater Providence area, becoming integrated into the wider socioeconomic circles of city society. In this manner, the Cape Verdean community evolved into a "hidden" minority in the region, having lost their territorially-based association.

For generations people have moved across oceans to take advantage of economic opportunities in America. Large-scale changes in technology throughout the nineteenth and twentieth centuries allowed investments to be made by people who created centers of development and channeled needed labor power into areas of high profits. The large-scale movement of people from primarily peripheral parts of Europe, Africa, and Asia caused families to separate while local systems of social and economic organization had to accommodate long-distance relationships or the end of relationships. The separation of people from their homelands and the unification of disparate migrants from the peripheries of the world in urban areas of poverty justified, for the dominant strata of American society, the inequities that emerged as immigrants became wage workers. New migrants start at the bottom and must work themselves up the ladder of success.

At the turn of the century, the New England textile and jewelry industries absorbed European rural folk, liberated from their work on the land and the pressures of the agrarian production cycle, so tied to unpredictable weather conditions and local economies. The period between 1870 and 1910 saw the most intense migration to Rhode Island. According to Mayer and Goldstein, the state's manufacturing employment during this period increased by 245 percent and its total workforce expanded by 284 percent (1958:9). Most people came from Ireland, French Canada, and the Portuguese Atlantic Islands: the Azores, Madeira, and Cape Verde. According to a recent study of Cape Verdean migration by Marilyn Halter, on the average 28 Cape Verdeans entered the United States every year between 1860 and 1887; 204.4 between 1889 and 1899; and 1,896 between 1900 and 1921. From 1921 to 1934, the average dropped to 142.4 people. Most came to New Bedford, although Providence was where many Cape Verdeans intended to settle (1986:10-11), travelling by rail to do so.

As competition from the South reduced Rhode Island's earlier industrial advantages in the textile market, the increased demand for textile production during the First World War reprieved this most critical industry from collapse and sustained Rhode Island's economic backbone for a while longer. The outbreak of the war limited the flow of immigrants, and the restrictions of 1917 through 1922 reduced immigration dramatically. During the interwar period the economic decline continued and the weakness of Rhode Island's industrial structure became apparent. That employment in the region depended on textile production is evidenced by the fact that manufacturing employment in Rhode Island dropped sixteen percent between 1919 and 1939, a period of major decline in the New England textile industry. In the whole country the decline in manufacturing employment was only three percent (ibid: 14). The Korean War followed and supported industrial employment in the state for a few more years.

As manufacturing employment declined, laborers moved into trade and service sectors. The slowdown of immigration to the United States and the inability of those already here to return home coincided with a change in which immigrants became ethnic Americans. Cape Verdeans were immobilized by the immigration laws, because even those who had valid United States passports feared that they might not be allowed to return after visiting the Islands. At this time, they increasingly experienced upward mobility into the consuming middle class, investing in a new American national consciousness. In this process people suppressed and de-emphasized cultural distinctions within ethnic groups, distinctions which back home might have separated one village or region from another or one island from another. The wars in Europe forced people to choose sides and brought ethnic Americans under suspicion if their nation of origin happened to be on the wrong side. This further repressed and at times kept hidden those cultural identities out of favor.

For much of this history, American society suffered the impact of prejudices, among which were the anti-alien movements of the last century. Strong sentiments against Southern and Eastern Europeans, Asians, and Catholics were unleashed against newly arriving immigrant groups. Government, advertising, business, and the media held up the white Anglo-Saxon Protestant cultural model as the American identity to which immigrant populations should aspire. The tensions created in homogenizing ethnic distinctiveness created countervailing tendencies. Groups fought to maintain and develop their identities in the face of pressures to conform. People's responses to these conflicting values diverged widely, resulting in a continuum of adaptations, from fully identifying and being identified as American to maintaining ethnic and national identities and traditions.

While a few Cape Verdeans were able to achieve upward mobility in the interwar years, they did so against resistance by racially prejudiced Americans. The post-World War II period brought about critical changes for Fox Point Cape Verdeans as economic opportunities increased and as their neighborhood underwent a radical transformation. Upward mobility became more attainable as dock work and merchant marining were in great demand, becoming financially lucrative. The economic opportunities for Cape Verdeans were part of a broad recovery for the United States that brought on major population shifts as urbanites moved into suburbs. The Irish of Fox Point did just that, leaving behind their old city neighborhood. Azorean Portuguese, too, left for other parts of the city and suburbs. Unlike the Irish, they were replaced by new Azorean immigrants to Fox Point, which thus sustained a vitality equalled only by Italian communities in Providence.

The depressed housing market came alive in this period as federal support allowed veterans of the wars to participate in the economic boom. Housing loans and higher education were subsidized by government. Fox Pointers sought to better themselves, to get out and away from the stigmatized low-rent, dilapidated, and old-style tenements that others called slums. When Fox Point was seen from the outside in, as returning soldiers might see it, the decrepit conditions of the neighborhood were brought into relief. As one fifty-year-old Cape Verdean put it, "I didn't know how bad off we were until I left Fox Point," a feeling shared among others in his generation.

The movement of ethnics out of Fox Point hardly meant the abandonment of the old neighborhood. Its proximity to Brown University and the Rhode Island School of Design and its appeal to artists, students, and professionals as the oldest neighborhood in the city and one of the most architecturally significant attracted entrepreneurs who raised rents. Thus property values climbed and the makeup of the neighborhood was totally transformed. The transition of the neighborhood at this time had its antecedents in parts of Fox Point outside the cluster of streets claimed by Cape Verdeans. The disintegration of the Irish community whose members lived in nearby streets had preceded urban renewal and was precipitated by the post-World War II mobility of urban white ethnics into suburbs. The desire to leave and the real estate pressures that made this possible also provided opportunities for Brown University expansion. Between 1950 and 1972, the proportion of Irish in the congregation of the once predominantly Irish St. Joseph's church fell to ten or twenty percent. The imminent collapse of the church was impeded only by the arrival of additional Catholic residents from other ethnic groups who had settled into Fox Point. The Irish had abandoned Fox Point.

Although Cape Verdeans were moving out of Fox Point even before the Second World War, few settled in the wealthier North Providence area. Many moved to East Providence, which they viewed as a cut above Fox Point and where other Cape Verdeans had already settled. South Providence was one of the least desirable areas to which Cape Verdeans moved, although many have done so in the last two decades primarily because rents were cheap. Although before 1950 South Providence was populated by an affluent middle class, since then the area has become known for low rents, absentee landlordism, and poverty. Housing projects, the oldest in the city, were located here as South Providence became the neighborhood for poor whites, African-Americans, new Spanish-speaking populations, and Southeast Asian refugees. A few racially mixed couples of the young urban middle class also came here to invest in the rehabilitation of run-down or abandoned homes. Put simply, Cape Verdeans with higher incomes moved to East Providence; those with lower incomes settled into South Providence.

Although Cape Verdeans dispersed into various neighborhoods and enclaves of greater Providence, many of them maintained social and cultural ties with Fox Point. They also continued to use the term "family" to express their relationship to each other and to their old community. Those who left earlier helped generate the push-pull forces of further neighborhood emigration. People saw family, friends, and neighbors move out, rents increase, and social life in the neighborhood change as new residents moved in. Soon even those who had hung on moved out too. A few Cape Verdeans still rented there and an even smaller minority had been able to purchase homes.

After World War II, earlier urban redevelopment plans were revived. By the 1960s South Main Street had been closed for a number of years, during which Cape Verdeans were forced to leave their housing. Three generations of the Islanders had made their homes there and when they left, anger and frustration displaced old neighborhood and ethnic pride.

When poor people are forced out of their neighborhoods as a result of political, economic, and social forces, richer people come to occupy the residences, and new shopping areas are created for the affluent. The process is called displacement and gentrification. Inherently this process is one of inequality, made even more perverse when the distinctions between these two populations are also defined by differences in color. The translation of color differentiations into racial categories invests the social and economic place of each population with a false notion that these distinctions are the "natural order" of things.

The process of displacement and gentrification was painful for the Cape Verdeans of Fox Point. The social deprivation they have suffered as a group some Cape Verdeans have likened to "grieving," what people feel when a member of the family has died. Moreover, the helplessness of being forced to move against their will and because of their skin color can only suggest a similarity to the forces that bring about genocide or ethnocide. Displacement of this type is a violent act. The impact of being uprooted can be more fully comprehended when the contradictions inherent in Cape Verdean multiple identities are understood.

As far as anyone knows, when Cape Verdeans came to the United States, they came as Portuguese. Immigration officials identified them as Portuguese because the state governing them prior to immigration was Portugal. This identity took on quite a different significance as they settled into New England among other Portuguese people. While their nationality was Portuguese, locally they were tagged as Portagee, Gee, and Brava.

Members of the first generation that created South Main culture tenaciously clung to their Portuguese identity. With it, they were identified as a people with a European tradition, separate from Black Americans. Separation from blackness was important among Cape Verdeans and preceded their adaptation to American society. Archibald Lyall discovered this years ago. He wrote, "Be it a Cape Verdean as black as ebony he strongly objects to being called black. He is a man of color, an 'Home de cor'; a 'blac' to him is a heathen from Africa" (1936:71). Despite their insistence, Cape Verdeans could not remove themselves from Black identity. In New England, they quickly became known as Black Portuguese, and this is how they came to be distinguished from African-Americans, the descendents of slaves, and from "White Portuguese" (Azoreans).

Among some Cape Verdeans, the feeling for a separate, non-Black identity ran deep and strong. One man in his forties told me that his mother "didn't like us associating with anyone but Cape Verdeans." Many Cape Verdeans, particularly those of this man's generation, express contempt for African-Americans, asserting that "they don't have family." Mothers played a critical role in nurturing the idea of Cape

Verdean distinctiveness in their children growing up in America. The reference to "family" here has meaning both in terms of relations of blood and marriage, kin, and in the larger, more global sense of ethnic community and the sharing of common values. African-Americans came to inhabit the same pockets of poverty in Providence as Cape Verdeans, as their numbers increased and as opportunity for unskilled work grew. Yet while they shared the impact of prejudice and poverty, Cape Verdeans fought to reproduce their cultural distinctiveness.

The predominantly white society had come to view Blacks as a population of rootless and uncultured people (Szwed 1972), characterizations that were equally abhorrent to Cape Verdeans. People of African descent perceived these slurs as added insults to those attitudes that have kept them from equally sharing opportunities for status and mobility in the United States. Descendents of American Blacks perceived Cape Verdeans as "uppity" and "snobbish." According to one man, "Cape Verdeans are still people of color, just like us." Cape Verdeans were perceived by American Blacks in Providence much like American Indians, as claiming non-Black identities in order to obtain resources made available to them by government programs. To African-Americans, being Black meant being subjected to the same kinds of class constraints to which descendents of slaves have had to conform.

The other population with which Cape Verdean identity has had affiliation has been the Portuguese (primarily Azorean) group that shared neighborhoods with them. Both underwent similar colonial and immigration histories, although Azoreans quickly differentiated themselves or were differentiated by others as "White Portuguese." Azoreans were made up of people brought together from Mediterranean Europe and Africa in Portugal's first plantation experiments and also played a role in the Yankee whaling industry. The Azoreans could not be identified as Bravas or Cape Verdeans. Since they were "white," they escaped the stigma to which Black Portuguese were subjected.

South Main culture, as it was created by the three generations of Fox Point Cape Verdeans since the turn of the century, was an amalgam of shared identity, history, and traditions forged from the distinctions that had existed among them on the various Cape Verdean Islands. The people from the different islands, despite cultural, psychological, and historical peculiarities, unified themselves in the neighborhood through their common experience as immigrants, laborers, and Blacks.

The events of World War II and thereafter brought about radical changes in their common identity. Shared experiences in segregated Black

63

military platoons, subjection to the discrimination of the wider society around them, and their common poverty and blocked mobility brought about a shift in identity, especially among the second and third generations. The Civil Rights movement and progressive laws in the 1960s provided further impetus for the acceptance of Black identity. The "Black is beautiful" and "roots" movements further supported common identity with African-Americans, bringing many Providence Cape Verdeans to actively engage in and at times to spearhead the civil rights struggles for greater justice and economic and social opportunities.

National liberation movements of colonized regions generated "Third Worldism" and intensified nationalism. Africans and African-Americans were vigorously involved in these movements, which reflected a wide political spectrum. Cape Verdeans could be found participating in both radical and conservative movements. For some, the emergence of the independent nation-state of Cape Verde in 1975 reinforced their African identity as expressed by the leaders of the homeland. Within a decade, the mainstream of Cape Verdeans in Providence had come to support the new government's economic development efforts. The Cape Verdean government, in turn, has made efforts to gain support from its diaspora and has actively courted Cape Verdean Americans in order to gain their continued financial, political, and spiritual support.

In the last two decades, the African wars of liberation generated a new set of immigrant Cape Verdeans, who are dissimilar in experience and world view to those who came at the turn of the century or who grew up in America since then. The droughts and troubled economy in Cape Verde perpetuated the continued flow of Cape Verdeans to New England, adding to the labor pool. Since 1965, when immigration laws allowed their entry again, and since 1975, when Cape Verde became independent, a new wave from Cape Verde has settled in the Providence area. As many as 10,000 Cape Verdeans of this newer migration now live in the city of Pawtucket, bordering Providence. The new migration has added a new dimension to the already complex set of Cape Verdean identities in the area. The community's complexity is further intensified by differing perspectives on Cape Verde's independence, such as pan-Africanism and socialism. These new issues have spilled over into the attitudes and actions of second- and third-generation Fox Point Cape Verdeans, as well.

The first-generation Cape Verdeans conserved homeland culture. They acted upon the values that were part of homeland life, while adapting to Fox Point conditions. Their former social distinctions were too subtle for Americans and so became less important to the Cape Verdeans in Fox Point. Differences in shade of skin color defined the difference between upper and lower social status in the islands. In America, people are either Black or white; no other social or color status was available to Cape Verdeans in the eyes of the larger American society. The availability of social hierarchy first within ethnic groups and neighborhoods and then in the context of society at large provided a complex arena of interaction. While white ethnics could take greater advantage of more choices and move out of their culture-bound, poor working-class neighborhoods, Black people almost universally found this difficult or impossible. Cape Verdeans could grow in social and economic esteem within their ethnic group, but like African-Americans they remained low-class as a group and were deprecated in society at large.

The subsequent lowering of the color barrier and the active recruitment of minorities reproduced a political clientelism similar to the *cumpad* (godparenthood) system on the docks and on the streets. Ward politics were rigidly governed by patronage and rooted in the social and political structures of neighborhoods, where family ties were critical to power and mobility and provided access to limited resources. The Democratic Party, supported by the Fox Point Irish, was at the heart of neighborhood politics as it was for the city as a whole. Cape Verdeans had worked out their relationships to this power structure early on. Those who had party connections obtained jobs in this manner. Federally-governed minority policies increasingly provided opportunities for Cape Verdeans, made Black identity more advantageous, and slowly created broader and quicker-paced opportunities for socioeonomic mobility.

The Civil Rights and Black Power movements further generated confidence in a Black identity. The reversal of earlier trends, where whiteness was invariably an advantage, brought more ambiguity into Cape Verdean ethnic identity. Cape Verdeans were, in actuality, eveything from "black" to "white" and increasingly, they had pushed into the middle income class. This has meant that in the last two decades, Cape Verdeans in the Providence area have ceased to fit the convenient and hegemonic classification of ethnic, racial, or class stereotyping of society at large and therefore have themselves participated in the forces that shattered the self-contained community built by Fox Point Cape Verdeans on South Main Street. Cape Verdeans today are filling roles in most sectors of Providence society.

While the "family" idiom is still invoked, the starker divisions signified by residence, Fox Point, East Side, East Providence, South Providence, and by occupation, physician, professor, longshoreman, civil servant, laborer, bring into question the continued viability of the patterns of interaction that once held together Fox Point Cape Verdeans. Despite this emergent heterogeneity and people's ambiguous and conflicting roles within it, most Cape Verdeans still wax nostalgic about the past South Main culture and insist that "then, we were all family!"

The vigor with which Cape Verdean identity was reinforced along historical, racial, cultural, social, economic, occupational, political, and residential lines began to disintegrate as mobility patterns for minorities began to fall into line with those accessible to other Americans. The differing advantages of being identified as Cape Verdean or Black impacted on the sense of community maintained by residents of Fox Point. The Black-led civil rights movement provided no incentive for Cape Verdean identity development, but it did for a Black identity among Cape Verdeans. Opportunities for social and economic advancement provoked the rejection of the neighborhood that outsiders readily identified as a "slum." Yet as long as people lived in Fox Point and the networks that sustained family relations continued to operate, the Fox Point Cape Verdean community sustained a central force combining cohesion, comfort, and political power.

These conditions provided cultural closure for Fox Point Cape Verdean society in which South Main culture dominated. Integration into society at large through African, African-American (Black), and European ethnic (Portuguese) identities, as well as a unique Cape Verdean one, provided new opportunities for identity development, particularly as United States racial and poverty policies were liberalized. Increasingly, Cape Verdeans became "ethnics," much like any of the other immigrant groups that came to America at the turn of the century.

Chapter 6

Slum Clearance and Blight Removal

Today's cities are riddled with what scientists characterize as "urban problems." Such problems include inner-city poverty and decay, crises in health and education, crime, and structural inequalities, among others. Modern-day urban problems stem from America's rapid industrialization and commercial development, the unpredictable movement of capital in and out of urban centers, and the episodic shifts in industrial and labor markets. These problems have been further exacerbated by disinvestment in manufacturing and housing. Early industrial centers have been unable to keep pace with new and modernizing plants in newly developing regions. As factories have moved out of city centers to urban peripheries, retail stores have fled inner cities and resurfaced in shopping malls to service middle-income suburbs. Urban real estate barons have allowed their inner-city properties to decay or have abandoned them entirely, leaving the unserviced shells to form belts and pockets of poverty.

Ironically, this very "degeneration" contained the seeds of massive urban renewal efforts to "reclaim" the abandoned properties and repopulate the deserted landscape with taxpayers who would help revitalize America's failing cities. As one of America's oldest industrial cities, Providence also became one of the first cities to experience the cycle of urban decline and subsequent urban renewal. Over the years, a number of plans were designed to demolish the "slums" and rebuild the inner city. While some of these plans were coming to fruition, those who wanted to preserve historic housing, citing the high cost of "slum clearance," presented alternative strategies for modernizing. In Providence the experiment proceeded apace, beginning in the northeastern part of the city's East Side. A large section of this neighborhood was razed in the 1950s. The Lippitt Hill Project, as it was called, eliminated a primarily African-American neighborhood and replaced it with a shopping and residential complex called University Heights. The loss of historic houses here and the potential of further losses in other areas of the renewal zone brought influential East Side Provinconians into play. As a result, parts of Fox Point, scheduled for renewal demolition, were saved.

Thus, that particular historic residential district was rescued, although the commercial sections, particularly South Main Street, were altered to conform to investors' needs. Some old clapboard buildings were replaced by concrete structures or small-scale housing projects. Preserving Colonial architecture steeped in New England's Yankee traditions became the focus of political activity that pitted a primarily affluent, white population against working poor Blacks.

Historic preservation, rather than traditional slum clearance, was the means by which Cape Verdeans were wrenched out of their homes and cut off from the nurturing social relations of their neighborhood. Fox Point Cape Verdeans watched this act of social violence as their familiar neighborhood dramatically changed before their eyes. Familiar landmarks were demolished, replaced, or altered, undermining the people's sense of neighborhood identity and integrity, not to mention residents' own sense of social continuity. The Fox Point Cape Verdean community, the neighborhood unit, as a social process of cultural reproduction and transmission, came to an end. Cape Verdeans experienced their sense of disadvantage by being dispossessed. This was exacerbated by the destruction of the unity for which they had struggled for one hundred years, as they were forced to witness the physical demolition of the area they called their community.

The transformation of South Main Street brought about dramatic cultural changes in the neighborhood as familiar neighborhood institutions were replaced one after another. Some people's homes, in which a generation of youngsters had been raised, were converted into boutiques;

used furniture stores gave way to restaurants; the familiar candy store in which neighborhood children whiled away hours of their time was lost to urban renewal. The list goes on. While new Fox Point neighbors developed new means for social interaction (or, as was often the case, accepted limited forms of interaction), the departure of most Cape Verdeans from their neighborhood along with the dismantling of their social and cultural institutions was an irreplaceable loss to the entire community. Preservationist economic development, according to preservationist ideology, arrested the decline of the old neighborhood, which, they argued, led to the rescue of historic architecture. That this brought an end to a distinct cultural and social entity known as the Fox Point Cape Verdean community was not an issue to those who were altering the human geography of the area. Such people reasoned that historic preservation and displacement were "natural" market forces working themselves out.

Programs for the clearance of slums in Providence began in 1935, when the Housing Division of the Federal Emergency Administration of Public Works (WPA) generated a study entitled *Proposed Slum Clearance and Housing Project for Providence: South Main-Wickenden District.* The previous year, the *Providence City Plan Commission's 21st Annual Report* made clear an intention for planned obsolescence in the residential development of declining commercial and industrial districts. The *Report* stated that "Only residences of the poorer sort will be built in business districts, and the failure of these latter districts to be developed in the manner for which they are zoned will inevitably result in areas of blight" (1935:3-4). Improving the housing and services in Fox Point, without forcing people to move out of their community, was not a possibility considered in planning the changes for this part of Providence.

According to the 1935 WPA report, "South Main and Wickenden Streets are located near one of the city's best residential areas and favored by the state Planning Board as a slum clearance project" (ibid: 4-5). Referring to a survey of slum areas in Providence prepared by the Family Welfare Society, the WPA report concurred with the "practical responsibility of making healthy-minded law abiding citizens from children whose whole outlook on life has been warped by such living conditions" (ibid:5). "Slum conditions," according to the report, "bring about economic decline, tax delinquencies, declining real estate prices, and a declining suitability in rehabilitating old buildings. Vacancies, too, increased proportionately with declining housing conditions" (ibid:7). The report did not discuss the causes that created the slum conditions in the first place.

The WPA report did provide a penetrating insight into the neighborhood's quality of life as it was perceived by officials, a viewpoint which seemed to be shared by the majority of the people of Providence. The target zone was described as being a long site, "irregular and fairly narrow (which) . . . cannot be regarded as unified neighborhood. . . . The present population is unstable and employment is irregular. Small low grade shops border the highways. The area, centrally located, is excellent for wage earners. . . . All points in the city can be reached by trolley or bus, and the principal shipping is within walking distance. . . . The stores and offices for the most part are very low grade, and many are now vacant. . . . In general, overcrowding conditions prevail in the area, the buildings setting directly on the street and little yard space being available. Cross streets and lanes are 10 to 15 feet wide, consequently only rooms fronting on the main streets have sufficient daylight and air" (ibid:10-13). The petty bourgeois perspective in this analysis was obviously developed to support and justify urban renewal, destined ideologically to marginalize even further the people who had settled in Fox Point. This form of analysis hardly searched for cause and effect in regional political and economic history, blaming instead the victims and by doing so dehumanizing their condition as "low grade," "irregular," "vacant," "overcrowded," and the like. The ease of dislocating dehumanized groups is a historical phenomenon with numerous modern examples, of which America's urban African-Americans are one.

Fire risks and hazardous conditions were the criteria used for condemning 156 buildings. Twenty-five percent of the 1,024 rooms were vacant and the rest housed 1,375 people of "mixed races" (ibid:14). The condemned area would see no major street changes, although some of the alleys and narrow "unsavory" gangways were to have been closed and others widened. A park was also going to be built in the area.

The reconditioned dwellings were planned to accommodate families with incomes of $1,000 to $1,700 per year. Semi-detached houses were to accommodate families with income of about $2,500. Twenty percent of a family's income, it was felt, was "a reasonable amount for expenditure for rent including heat" (ibid: 17). While this consideration was fair for those with moderate incomes, it did not take into account the people who were residing there, nor the social violence that planned changes would cause those who would have to leave. This population's average annual family income was $1,133 in 1933. Half of the families earned less than $1,000, and one-quarter earned about $1,500 (ibid).

Leaving aside the reaction of those who were displaced, the plan was

70

attractive because it could provide access between the city center and outlying areas; it provided housing for a more affluent population; it raised property values and generated more taxes for the city; and it was expected to create jobs in a depressed area though construction and commercial activities. Yet the lives of the former residents were not considered. The assumptions upon which development plans were based clearly found the social relations and cultural values of Cape Verdeans in Fox Point irrelevant, and not just because the plans were aimed at saving properties rather than preserving a cultural context. Indeed, little thought was given to supporting the redevelopment of a neighborhood or of community life for the Cape Verdeans who were to be removed.

The Depression and the labor-intensive war years did not allow the WPA plan to be implemented, although it was not forgotten. In 1946, the Providence City Plan Commission adopted the *Master Plan for Redevelopment and Residential Area*, the *Master Plan for Thoroughfare*, and the *Master Plan for Land Use and Population Distribution*. In 1948, the City Council agreed with these findings. The zones with a "preponderance of blight" were officially designated as "Redevelopment Areas." In 1949, the proper zoning ordinances were passed. The City Plan Commission pointed to seventeen areas in which "blight" was defined as areas needing redevelopment; the South Main Street area was included as a primary target. In 1950, the Providence Redevelopment Agency prepared a *Tentative Plan for South Main Project Area D-8A*, based on the WPA's and subsequent studies.

The 1950 study showed that out of 193 dwelling units in the project area, seven were vacant. Another twelve had deteriorated to such a degree that they could not be occupied. Yet other units were used for storage purposes. The 186 occupied units housed 195 families. In total, 700 lived in the project area, 580 family members and 120 roomers and lodgers. Forty-three percent of the families consisted of one or two individuals, according to the Tentative Plan study (1950: 2). Virtually all the buildings were considered old: 86 percent had been constructed before 1900, 49 percent were over 100 years old, and 17 of the buildings had been erected before 1800 (ibid: 2-3). Cape Verdeans I interviewed some thirty years after the study appeared felt that many more people had lived in these buildings than were counted and pointed out that people listed as "individuals" were often members of larger households—an example would be a single person living with a family—rather than isolated persons living in rooming houses.

The street patterns reflected former uses inherited by Cape Verdean settlers. South Main Street remained a primary artery linking downtown Providence, the shore of Narragansett Bay, and southeastern Massachusetts. The *Providence Traffic Engineer Reports* mention that the project area had for years presented many "difficult problems" with regard to proper traffic control. The traffic accident rate between 1945-1950 here was twelve times the citywide rate (ibid: 3).

Institutions occupying non-residential buildings that were slated for closing included a fire station, a Central Boys' Club, Volunteers of America, the Salvation Army, a Barker Foundation storage area, and a garage leased by the United States Post Office. No mention was made of the rented Longshoremen's Union Hall, however. Eighty-four business establishments were counted in the project area. Second-hand stores were the most numerous of the retail stores, and plumbing and heating supply houses dominated the wholesaling group (ibid: 4). Many of the buildings that were used as business locations or had combined business/residential uses, according to the 1950 report, had a "detrimental effect on remaining dwelling units" (ibid: 4). That is to say, landlords reinvested little in such buildings, inducing neighboring landlords to use similar strategies for their buildings in order to maximize their profits or at least not incur losses.

The 1950 report concurred with the social and cultural evaluation of 1935. Researchers asserted that "many of our social ills are caused in large part by sub-standard physical conditions . . . (contributing) to the exceedingly high incident rate of communicable disease, the disproportionate number of illegitimate children born within the area, the excessive number of criminal arrests and juvenile delinquency cases, and the large number of traffic personal injury accidents" (ibid: 5). The City Department of Health agreed and noted that "this area . . . (was) definitely below standard and that it should be cleared and rebuilt" (ibid: 6). According to the report, there appeared to be "definite evidence of overcrowding, improper sanitation, and improper housing facilities in the South Main Street Project Area." The report concluded "that steps should be taken immediately to prepare proper housing facilities for the low income and transient population at present in that area" (ibid). Of the dwelling units surveyed, eighty-five percent were considered slum units because of unsafe and unsanitary conditions, five percent were listed as "adequate," and ten percent were held to be in "doubtful" condition. In contrast to the condition of the South Main site, a survey was carried out on the Benefit Street frontage north of Transit Street, a healthy residential area next to Fox Point, where environment and dwelling units scored ninety-three percent "adequate" and none were designated slums (ibid: 6-7). As far as the commercial properties, it was stated that "most of the 54 retail establishments are marginal enterprises." The Benefit Street architecture was at the heart of the historic preservation effort, although, according to Fox Pointers, these buildings were as physically "bad off" as some of those in the redevelopment area.

It must be clear from the nature of the reports and the way in which they were written that the author's perceptions concerning this settlement and the housing located there were colored by a variety of interests and historical factors. According to the Redevelopment study, clear-cut reasons existed for selecting South Main as a project area. Among them was that it was a blighted area and it was immediately adjacent to good-quality residential and commercial areas whose decline was imminent, a sort of domestic domino theory. It was a slum, but well situated in the context of a developing urban civic center and an exclusive residential area, as well as abutting a large educational enterprise, Brown University.

A need for additional housing for middle-class taxpayers was the project's self-described justification. The resolution to the problem was suggested as the "clearance and redevelopment of the area and the provisioning of more housing units than it displaces, doubling it in the case of South Main, although the units are not to be in the same economic range as those existing" (ibid: 10). Provisions were made for the families now living in this slum area by providing housing outside the area or in low-rent housing developments (ibid). However, people who used to live in close proximity found themselves separated from each other by the new housing conditions. And while some of the buildings in the old neighborhood could be saved and the ambience of some mythical past could be recreated, the genuine community dynamic of the ethnic and working-class neighborhood that had emerged over the century since the wealthy abandoned the waterfront was not a value factored into the development process. The viewpoint which holds that the cultural and social needs of a community are important units of social organization that must be preserved was given no consideration.

The justification for displacing and relocating the Fox Point residents is not clearly argued in the plan, although the study points out that "the relocation problem in this area is small as compared to other slum blighted areas in the city" (ibid: 11). As far as the planners were concerned, "slum dwellers" were homogenous and had similar problems. They were Black and therefore poor. This assumption gave rise to another: that the people living in Fox Point would be better off if they

73

were moved. That diversity might exist in such areas of economic decline and that people chose to stay close to kith and kin, despite their economic capacity to live somewhere else, played little or no role in the planning and implementation of the redevelopment project. Two other arguments were made in support of the plan: first, some housing units had deteriorated and were vacated; second, some housing units were being used for non-residential purposes. Significantly, the units were not as overcrowded as other deteriorated areas typically were, and in fact, according to planning reports, a high proportion of the families consisted of one or two people. In the final analysis, the quality of the residences and of the uses to which the buildings were put, as judged by government officials, planners, and developers, was the determining factor in revitalization plans.

Financial gains for the area as a whole were emphasized in the studies. Slum clearance, for those who supported the ideological premises of this type of development project, was the panacea permitting new investment to take place. Slum clearance and urban reinvestment, it was asserted, would "protect the adjacent areas of high quality, and also enhance their value" (ibid), a domino theory working in reverse. Of all the project areas, South Main was to go first, synchronized with that section of Fox Point where the freeway and access roadway had priority (ibid). The freeway and South Main redevelopments were linked because the freeway was to divert traffic and channel it away from South Main to reduce clogged traffic arteries, while allowing better access to downtown as well as around it.

In-town apartment housing would make South Main Street attractive to private capital. This was also compatible with the needs of the city since "it would produce the greatest volume of private investment and consequently the greatest potential tax revenue" (ibid). Multiple housing held the area's highest and best re-use potential, although according to the plan, "commercial redevelopment was always possible" (ibid), pending the placement of the freeway. The reports are quite clear that the poor and those who chose to live in an ethnic, working-class community blocked the designs for a healthy, revitalized area close to downtown. The social and cultural life in the designated area was perceived as an obstacle to the planners' visions. The lifestyle of the poor did not allow for development and revitalization. Capital investments would serve a new population, not the poorer Cape Verdeans who had been living there for years. It was clear that government officials and developers worked very hard to remove this obstruction.

The modernization of South Main and Wickenden Streets must be viewed from the perspective of Providence development as a whole. In the 1950s through the 1960s, the Providence metropolitan area lagged in population growth compared with similar older cities in the United States. Providence experienced a population loss of seventeen percent in this period, continuing a trajectory of population decline begun in the 1930s. This decline reflects the city's inability to attract and maintain industrial employers and keep city dwellers from moving to the suburbs (Brown, Harris, Stevens, Inc., 1963). The decline and impoverishment of old industrial cities in the United States was caused by systematic disinvestment. This in turn motivated the attempt to rescue the cities through government-directed and -sponsored programs. The forced movement and dispersion of the working poor and the impoverished of inner cities resulted.

Although a thirty-eight percent gain in non-white population was experienced between 1950 and 1960, the lack of jobs and adequate housing maintained the city's non-white population at a mere six percent in 1963 (ibid: 3). Moreover, Providence showed an increase in the sixty-five and over age groups, experiencing substantial losses in the most vigorous and productive age group, from eighteen to sixty-five. Providence was getting poorer and older, a process that corresponded to a need for public and low-income housing. Finally, in this period Providence experienced a decreasing household size; in 1950, the average was 3.26 persons and in 1960 there was an average of 2.95 persons per household. This decline is accounted for by the increase in single-person households, with the greatest population losses in low-rent areas (ibid: 3-5).

Residential patterns reflect employment opportunities. The decline in the predominant category of manufacturing employment continued into the 1950-1960 period and has persisted through today. In this decade, the textile industry alone suffered a 53.8 percent decline in employment, from 60,600 to 28,000, and although government employment increased 150 percent in this period, from 15,986 to 40,000, it could not replace the lost jobs. Employment increases in the finance, insurance, and real estate sectors also took place, growing from 9,314 to 13,000 jobs (ibid: 6). As demand for unskilled workers declined, demand for professional and skilled work increased. A marked shift from production to service and sales jobs correlates to a shift of population from old, declining urban areas to newly built or rebuilt housing in suburbs and luxury housing areas in the city. The result of residential shifts was that by 1963 the annual per capita income in the city was only $2,119 (ibid: 9), with the majority of the city's population remaining unskilled and earning low wages.

75

Chapter 7

Manny Almeida's Ringside Lounge

"Nigger removal," as Cape Verdeans called displacement, was not passively accepted by them. Cape Verdeans refused to totally give up their neighborhood. Between 1964 and 1980, a variety of arenas of struggle came into being, but it was Manny Almeida's Ringside Lounge that emerged as the last center of Fox Point Cape Verdean resistance. It is here that "people returned to their roots," according to one man—that is, Manny's became the last beachhead of Fox Point Cape Verdean culture. It was here that Fox Point Cape Verdean ethnic consciousness was highest.

In 1964, Manny Almeida's Ringside Lounge was relocated from a downtown location to a "strategic" corner in Fox Point. As pointed out earlier, people in the city quickly came to refer to it as a "Black" or "Cape Verdean" bar, even though the owner was an Azorean Portuguese and despite the predominantly non-Cape Verdean population that surrounded the old Cape Verdean portion of the neighborhood. For the Cape Verdeans who came to frequent it and for the predominantly white middle-class people involved in modernizing the neighborhood and who remembered Providence in the 1950s or earlier, Manny's corner was seen as a symbolic remnant of what South Main Street had been. Both groups wanted the location for themselves. For Cape Verdeans, it was the one remaining locus of "family," a place in the old neighborhood where the Cape Verdeans could keep alive the memory which embodied the experience of an immigrant community. For others (the mostly white developers, commercial entrepreneurs, preservationists, and the general public that passed by the corner on their way to and from work or shopping) it was just one more place to be saved from the deterioration of its former slum status. The latter group found Blacks hanging out on the corner "unpleasant," "troublesome," and by definition an unacceptable reminder of the decline of the recent past, as defined by those white middle-class people who desired rapid changes in the neighborhood. This, too, was symbolic in that "blackness" represented a threat whose perception may be traced to the origins of modern Western traditions (cf. Robinson 1983).

The corner was seen as "shabby" since the buildings around it, like the Lounge, were not being kept up. While the sidewalk on the corner had been replaced with a "nice" herringbone design of laid bricks, sections had been pulled up and the sand underneath could be found all over the street. Despite periodic sweeping of the corner, bottles and litter were visible most of the time. The Black men "hanging out" in front did not give white, middle-class passers-by a sense of confidence in the area. Most whites tended to avoid the corner, except those who lived in the area or those who understood that there was nothing to fear.

The transformation of South Main and Wickenden Streets pushed the remaining Cape Verdean residents into the less drastically altered eastern portion of the neighborhood. A few even managed to purchase houses or secure apartments in the old neighborhood. Those who moved away often returned to visit family, friends, and neighbors. This was done with such frequency that in actuality the part of Wickenden Street where Manny's was located still "belonged" to the Cape Verdeans.

The same forces that displaced Cape Verdeans had displaced the downtown Ringside Tap, the tavern owned by Manny Almeida before he moved his establishment to Fox Point. Thus a certain irony in the forces of displacement brought Manny Almeida to open a bar in the Fox Point neighborhood. He had been forced to move when the building in which the bar had been located was torn down to become a parking lot. According to some of the Fox Pointers, he then had a stroke and during his recovery opened Manny's. When Manny's Lounge was opened, he purchased a bar in the nearby city of Warwick as well, tending it himself while employing another person to manage the Lounge in Fox Point. At the end of each day he drove home to Fox Point and picked up the daily receipts.

Manny Almeida was a "White Portuguese" (Azorean) and well known as a Providence fight promoter. Some of the locals say that "he brought boxing to Providence" and "he had made Marciano great." He owned a boxing ring and gym in Fox Point where many Cape Verdeans used to work out. A few, like George Aroujo, became locally well-known professionals. Among Cape Verdeans, feelings about Manny were mixed and contradictory. Those who trained with him spoke fondly of those times. Others, Cape Verdeans and non-Cape Verdeans alike, thought him racially biased, although people spoke of him as "a nice guy." According to one man who worked for him at the Lounge, "when Manny's wife died, he had Black pallbearers," indicating his broadmindedness. Manny Almeida's reputation in boxing and Cape Verdean involvement in his boxing ring drew Cape Verdeans to his bar, although it is not certain whether Manny actually wanted them to come. While no one in Fox Point ever said he wanted to attract only his Azorean countrymen who lived in the densely packed three-decker neighborhood, people did hear him say at times, "I want Blacks out."

The ambiguity felt about Manny Almeida and the ambiguity he perhaps felt about other people is not unusual given the frequent face-to-face interaction in a relatively closed community. Absolute feelings and statements about anyone in Fox Point were readily disputed and modified rapidly. Kinship, friendship, and neighborhood ties, and contexts in which people were forced to be interdependent for lack of adequate resources, were the dynamic ingredients that produced ambiguous feelings. The ambiguity of relationships was part and parcel of social and cultural life.

Toward the end of the South Main displacement period, before Manny's Lounge was opened on Wickenden Street in 1964, the corner storefront was an Irish bar called Sullivan's. When most of the Irish moved out of the neighborhood, the bar closed down, although another Irish bar a few blocks east on Wickenden had continued to attract a clientele. When Manny's opened where Sullivan's used to be, Cape Verdeans came to frequent the bar almost exclusively. For some, going there to drink was a pactical issue "since if you got drunk, you didn't have far to stagger home," according to one client. Only a few Cape Verdeans could actually do this because only a few lived in Fox Point. If you did have to stagger home, no matter how far you had to go, "there'd be someone there to help." Cape Verdeans came here to drink because Manny's and the neighborhood were familiar to them. They knew that no matter what happened here, it was in the context of a predictable environment that made them feel safe, acceptable, and protected.

Other bars were located in the neighborhood, but none was as popular as Manny's with the Cape Verdean crowd. Displaced Cape Verdeans continued to frequent the neighborhood, almost as if they were still living there. The bar was a success and Manny, not a well man, adapted to the lucrative turn of events by hiring Cape Verdeans to manage the place. This further supported the Cape Verdean clientele. The bartenders drew patrons from their personal social networks and since the people hired were well-liked, the bar became a success; this is how Cape Verdeans took it over. They established their predominant patronage at Manny Almeida's Ringside Lounge, continuing until the bar's closing in 1980.

Manny's became more significant in 1971, when Dave's Grill opened next door. Neighborhood people had been calling it the Spa since the time it opened on South Main Street, "God knows when," according to one man. John had operated the Grill since 1951, when he bought it after getting out of the Navy. He had moved the little restaurant a number of times before opening next to Manny's. Like the Lounge, the clientele of the small single-counter restaurant was almost exclusively Cape Verdean. John had become "family" in Fox Point ever since he bought the Spa. He had to move a number of times while on South Main Street, before it really became popular at its location next to the Boys' Club and the Longshoremen's Union Hall, both popular Cape Verdean hangouts. Over the years, John's relationship to the Cape Verdeans became so close that it was common for one or two of the customers, seeing John busy with other matters, to take orders, cook, and to serve themselves and others.

In between jobs, the Cape Verdean longshoremen frequently had to wait for work and so they came to the Spa or Manny's to play cards, discuss the news of the day, relay information, play the numbers, read the paper, eat, and drink. The nature of longshoremen's work and the way in which jobs were acquired made hanging out critical to longshoremen's lives and both Dave's and Manny's were adapted to that purpose. Retired men also came to Dave's to play cards, an activity in which John was a wholehearted participant. The older men found good company here and whiled away many otherwise lonesome hours. Local politics always played a significant role in their conversation as they read and discussed the news of the day.

As Manny's grew in importance to Cape Verdean longshoremen, the part of Wickenden where South Main Street used to intersect, now part of Route 195, became an extension of South Main development. The street on which Manny's was located was being changed from rundown buildings and shops to an upscale shopping area interspersed with restored buildings housing lawyers' and doctors' offices and other new businesses, as well as providing residences for students and professionals. The new shops were frequented by antique buyers, gourmet cooking enthusiasts, and people interested in folk art, student furnishings and supplies, and natural foods. The restaurants and night spots found wide appeal, particularly among the college crowd.

The changes taking place in Fox Point brought the issue of race and ethnicity into play. As far as white people were concerned, Manny's and the Spa were places where Black people congregated. White neighborhood merchants and residents frequented the establishments, but rarely broke through the barrier of family intimacy. For Cape Verdeans, the establishments gave them a sense of belonging that was rooted in the experiences of the past. Being there meant their continued presence in Fox Point as a community. The meeting of friends, neighbors, and kin in a friendly atmosphere actualized for them their sense of common identity and unity in their neighborhood.

The association of the "blighted" South Main area with "slum" conditions by developers and planners, combined with a visibly African-American or Cape Verdean population that was interpreted as "stigmatizing" the exclusiveness of the East Side by the same people, shaped the public's acceptance of the inevitability of radical change. The elimination of slum conditions was the solution for rescuing the area from decay and socioeconomic decline. That a pocket of such highly visible signs of underdevelopment in Fox Point—symbolized by Manny's and Dave's as establishments that drew a Black clientele—was an irritant to those who preferred to have affluent families, professionals, and related businesses move in instead.

In addition to this state of bias, there was the problem of the Cape Verdeans' relationship to the Holy Rosary Roman Catholic Church, whose parishioners were primarily ethnic (Azorean) Portuguese. Over the years, Cape Verdeans had increasingly stopped attending Holy Rosary because they felt unwelcome. Some have said that the racial views expressed there forced them to disassociate themselves from the Roman Catholic Church entirely. This may explain why the Faith Community Parish, a nearby Protestant church, established itself as a Cape Verdean mission and became popular among Fox Point Cape Verdeans. Reinforcing their disassociation from the church was Holy Rosary's role in displacing Cape Verdeans from the neighborhood. The houses around the front part of the church were demolished as part of urban renewal and to make possible the establishment of a parochial school which was supposed to have served Fox Point's Portuguese speakers. All buildings except one, which belonged to a Cape Verdean octogenarian, were razed and the land was transferred to the Providence Redevelopment Agency, which in turn sold it to the church for a nominal sum. To add insult to injury, the land cleared of one-time Cape Verdean homes became a fenced-in, asphalted parking lot that was unused except on Sundays, feasts, and other large-scale ritual occasions. No school was ever built.

Manny's was located between the church and the area where most of the Fox Point Azoreans lived. People had to walk by Manny's to get to church and return home. Complaints of improprieties and even an occasional violent episode put neighborhood pressure on the bar's owner to curtail his business. According to local understanding, when Manny died in 1975, his executor allowed the bar to degenerate and then sold it to an immigrant, "greenhorn" Azorean. The matter of the bar and its "seedy" character became of such significance in the neighborhood that people organized to close it down. Illicit activities, probably no more or less than in other non-Cape Verdean areas in Fox Point, were said to take place in Manny's; prostitution, numbers playing, gambling, and drug selling were said to have been rampant. I saw none of these during my stay.

Cape Verdeans perceived the intensely bad feelings about Manny's as an issue that revolved around race and class. They understood that the political and economic forces which determined if they worked or not and where they could live and not live were not under their control. Most people perceived Manny's corner as an island of "Black Portuguese" in a fundamentally white neighborhood. Moreover, those who frequented Manny's had experienced the permanence of their low socioeconomic position in a predominantly white-controlled society and understood how difficult it was for them to acquire political ascendency. However, Cape Verdeans also understood the "power" of unity, even if only in the subtle context of Manny Almeida's Ringside Lounge. In any event, all parties agreed on one thing: the significance of Manny's clearly lay in the presence of Cape Verdeans.

Not all Cape Verdeans felt that Manny's was a positive element in the neighborhood. Some politically active intellectuals felt that Manny's Cape Verdean clientele represented an unattractive element in their ethnic group and generally disassociated themselves from the bar, although they frequented Dave's Cafe next door. Despite this reservation, the general feeling about the importance of Manny's in the neighborhood brought one man to say: "For Cape Verdeans, if there wouldn't be a Manny's, they'd have to invent one!" The symbolic aspect of Manny Almeida's Ringside Lounge did not escape at least some of the Cape Verdeans of Fox Point. They understood that their presence there served as a reminder to everyone that Cape Verdeans remained in "their" neighborhood!

For those who were interested in protecting or increasing their property values, Manny's was an eyesore, a public nuisance and disturbance which prevented further development. For some people, the continued presence of perceived low-income Blacks was physically and economically threatening. For Cape Verdeans, Manny's represented a sustaining foothold in the neighborhood where they felt at home. The expansion of the middle-class, white "East Side" into Fox Point, in terms of class and color, reinforced the historic socieconomic disparity between the two neighborhoods. The opulent wealth represented by Brown University was painfully obvious to Cape Verdeans, in contrast to the economic status of Fox Point immigrant and worker populations. While finding Fox Point itself "quaint," according to one resident, "East Siders tended to frown upon Fox Pointers," the ethnic populations who lived there.

East Side people were virtually forced to drive by Manny's since it was located on a major artery between downtown Providence and their neighborhood. As people who have had little to do with low-income Blacks, they found the presence of groups of Blacks so close to work and residence frightening or uncomfortable. East Siders commonly remarked about the discomfort they experienced when walking in "that" part of Fox Point, at times expressing their amazement over my ability to carry out research there.

Paradoxically, fear of the unknown and the different did not always characterize East Side attitudes toward Manny's Cape Verdean clientele. The 1960s, for example, were considered a liberating period in America, with profound impact. Students, faculty, and administrators from Brown University regularly came down the Hill and mingled with Manny's crowd. Even Brown University's president was said to have patronized the bar. Looking back, Cape Verdeans and former students both warmly recall their mutually satisfying interaction, although they emphasize different recollections. Cape Verdeans always focused on the interesting discussions carried out at the bar, while former students talked about illicit (exotic) activities such as drug use and sales, prostitution, and fistfights.

The 1960s in Fox Point were an important period of transition for Cape Verdeans who continued to seek a base in their old neighborhood. Initially, Manny Almeida's Ringside Lounge was not the only spot or means for doing this. There were other significant gathering places as well. One was "Poor People's Park," created as "a sort of social club," according to one of its founders. It was located in the same street-level storefront that had housed the popular Three Lantern Bar, later razed to build the church parking lot. One cold and rainy day, a group of men "just took it over after looking for a place to hang out" and share some drink. Later, the space was legally acquired through political connections, entitling the informal group to rent the property for one dollar annually. Poor People's Park contained an upright piano, tables and chairs, and the usual paraphernalia of a club, except that all the plumbing had been ripped out by someone trying to make a little money by selling scrap. It was not an exclusively men's or adult club. Lots of people came: men, women, and children attended informal community gatherings. A story hour for kids was arranged and Cape Verdean music was performed; "it was truly a place for families to gather," according to one person who participated.

One of the organizers said, "it was very popular because it was something not intentionally done." Another person suggested, "People came in and knew they were establishing it, for nothing. People played Cape Verdean music there on a regular basis and everyone was family!" The people who made Poor People's Park a success also went to Manny's down the block.

One day in the early 1970s, Poor People's Park was demolished. Apart from the occasional illegal and short-lived after-hours clubs in Fox Point, Manny's truly became the last Cape Verdean hangout in the neighborhood. At the same time Cape Verdeans were seeking to maintain their connection to the neighborhood, two different housing corporations were formed to benefit the low- and moderate-income families of Fox Point. One of the groups was organized around Democratic ward politics and succeeded in administering a grant that brought four low-income family houses into being. These were sold to neighborhood Cape Verdean and African-American families at a cost they could afford.

The other group coalesced around the Fox Point Community Organization (FPCO), which struggled to obtain land from the city or from Brown University on moral grounds. Brown University in particular has been called on to compensate the displaced community. The institution was viewed as responsible for pushing people out because it was a large landowner and was engaged in campus expansion, student body growth, and control over the local economy. The Fox Point Community Organization's campaign in the neighborhood included skirmishes with absentee landlords who chose to rent apartments to groups of students at three times the rent that low- or moderate-income families could afford. Such practices drove up the cost of housing and increased taxes for everyone. They also contributed to the high rate of displacement caused by urban renewal.

The Fox Point Community Organization (FPCO) was able to help bring about the Fox Point Manor housing project for the elderly, where many old Fox Point Cape Verdeans live today. The FPCO also was successful in stemming Brown University's expansion into the neighborhood and made its administrators more conscious of the institution's impact there. During 1979-1980, the FPCO became virtually a Cape Verdean organization and as a result served to heighten awareness among Cape Verdeans of their strong identity with Fox Point and the significance of the neighborhood in their individual and collective histories. The transformation crystallized the division in the community between the interests of Cape Verdeans and Azoreans, as well as the division between those who believed in the value of social over market relations and those who promoted historic preservation efforts to mask social engineering of the environment and to increase real estate values. A number of cultural programs were organized, including ethnic festivals, in an effort to create more neutral conditions under which social problems common to ethnic groups could be addressed and an effective strategy could be formed. While the festivals themselves were popular and well attended, cooperation in common political arenas did not result. A CETA- and Rhode Island Committee for the Humanities-supported videotape project and a series of public forums publicized the injustices associated with displacement and gentrification both in the neighborhood and throughout the city. Their impact was limited to providing a voice for the powerless.

Manny's Ringside Lounge catered to a diverse clientele of Cape Verdeans from South Providence, East Providence, and Mount Hope, in addition to the few remaining Fox Pointers and more dispersed elements from other areas of the region. Virtually all Cape Verdeans who came to Manny's had some longshoreman connections; someone in the family worked on the docks. The second- and third-generation Cape Verdeans—whether local political figures, educators, administrators, unskilled workers, or unemployed—all came to Manny's and interacted with each other. Women came in the evenings, usually in the company of men. Youths and children came to play the jukebox and pinball machine after school and in the early evenings. They came by themselves and with adults. Although it was the men who dominated Manny's and drank there on a regular basis, it was considered by most Cape Verdeans a "family bar."

Chapter 8

Conclusions

Rhode Islanders fondly refer to Providence as a "big village." As a small city and one of the oldest urban centers in the country, it did have a variety of ethnically defined neighborhoods created by the global migrations of the nineteenth and twentieth centuries. But it was not the fact that most people of Providence were able to trace their roots to an agrarian past that gave the "village" concept its validity. Neither did the notion refer to the sometimes insular social systems that ethnic neighborhoods developed over the years, although these were important in maintaining ethnic distinctions. Instead, the "village" idea refers to the face-to-face interaction of daily life, a social condition in which actual or fictive kin, friends, and neighbors made up the basis of social interaction. As people in Providence used to say, "you can get more done through who you know, than what you know."

Public resources, in particular, became available through kin-based networks, embedded in the larger social system and replicated in the politics of neighborhoods that still dominate the body politic of urban ethnic-based communities. Patron-client relationships that commonly evolved out of "godparenting"—in the case of the Cape Verdeans—or similar social mechanisms created the linkages between the dominant, centralized political apparatus and the neighborhoods for the purpose of redistributing resources. Neighborhoods that developed unity along ethnic lines were successful in forging the correct chain of social relations that led to broader political power and economic resources. Conversely, for most people, formal bureaucratic channels interfered with getting things done, so people spent a great deal of time cultivating networks that created the *potential* for resource acquisition, a potential that could be reliably harvested at any time.

People who perceived the limited availability of resources understood that access to them, the distribution of jobs, housing, and other benefits of federal, state, and local programs, was gained only through social networks. The ties of kinship and friendship, against a background of neighborliness and patronage, were used and manipulated to circumvent the structures that had been set up—at least formally—to provide relatively equal access to resources, but in reality functioned to the advantage of some individuals rather than others. The large number of jobs available in the Providence city and the Rhode Island state governments, combined with the scarcity of other secure and well-paying jobs, strengthened the power and place of the patronage system in local society. Simply put, when resources were scarce, what some people were able to obtain through patronage they successfully kept out of the hands of others who were perhaps more deserving. By politically supporting kith and kin, friends and neighbors, the socioeconomic networks that provided normal access to resources were protected, strengthened, and reproduced, and this reinforced the traditional cohesion of neighborhoods, ethnic groupings, and communities, at which levels of social organization government resources were distributed.

This awareness of limited access to resources permeated social relations and reinforced the significance of ethnically defined communities and neighborhoods where residents sought and found conduits through which resources could be obtained. When one avenue was blocked, others were explored. For most residents of contemporary Providence, the coincidence of ethnicity, race, and class with community and neighborhood was a commonly recognized fact of life. The people who were able to manage the social dynamics of this coincidence on a significantly large scale were able to catapult themselves into power and thus provide advantages to their constituents. It was commonly believed, for example, that if an Italian received an important city job in Providence it was due to the fact that the mayor and 40 percent of the population were Italian, and not because the person was qualified for the job. Most people assumed that a direct relationship existed between one's individual economic welfare and the political ascendency of one's ethnic group. The strength of such conviction, that ethnicity can be politically advantageous, was often carried to extremes. One high-ranking non-Italian city bureaucrat appointed to his post by the Italian mayor, for example, went so far as to prominently display pictures of Frank Sinatra in his office to create affinity where none existed.

The absence of networks to link family, ethnic group, neighborhood, and community was widely perceived as an obstacle to legitimacy and success. As one administrator remarked, non-Rhode Islanders coming into the state "must pay their dues first and prove themselves" before access to resources would be available. "Paying dues" meant that people had to prove themselves reliable, dependable, and consistent. As indicated earlier, access to resources was based on these widely accepted notions, while local and regional ranking followed the contours of social and economic integration. Ethnicity, race, class, and neighborhood determined these contours and hence positions within regional social hierarchies that always embodied the potential for antagonisms along these lines of group identity.

For those who belonged to small or lower-ranked groups, networking could become crucial to social and economic survival. Group size, of course, was not everything, and this was true for Providence. Placement of economically and politically prominent and powerful members, particularly of small communities, was crucial to even entering the struggle for resources, since participation was determined by "paying one's dues." Generally speaking, those on the bottom included the most recent arrivals since they were in the process of paying their dues. Those refusing or unable to play the game, or those uninterested in paying dues, were quickly marginalized. And non-whites had their mobility further blocked by the color line.

Color, in this regard, had played an important role in the way people perceived the strength and quality of particular communities, with "white" usually pitted against "Black," while others landed somewhere in between. The perception of one's color or ethnic background as a determining characteristic of identity is a product of cultural formation. It is common—though misguided—for people to invent a biological justification for the pecking order which plays itself out in political and economic arenas. The popularly held beliefs concerning the inferiority of people of color allowed those who identified with dominant society to be complacent when government and private concerns manipulated the environments of Blacks to their detriment. The subsequent lack of resources and obstructed access to socioeconomic mobility crystallized tensions along ethnic and color lines and brought into greater relief a predominant idea among the elite, who made and carried out policies, that such conditions were predetermined by "biological" factors beyond human control.

As more opportunities became available in the economy and as governments formally supported the reduction of societal ethnic and racial prejudices through the Civil Rights movement, socioeconomic mobility increased and ethnic solidarity began to fade. Whenever resources diminished, however, and access to what remained was limited, the fight along all those lines through which access to resources was traditionally attainable was intensified anew. In Providence, ethnicity and race were the fallback mechanisms to be mobilized. The concentration of ethnic and racial groups in residential areas also made neighborhood identity a crucial element in gaining access to resources. Occupational and associational identities, when organized on the basis of ethnicity, race, or neighborhood, were also instrumental in political organizing for resources. These traditional divisions prevented common working-class identities from being acknowledged and made more difficult the struggle against the general pattern of oppression, especially during cyclical downturns in the economy, when class-wide solidarity would have benefited all members of the working class.

Most Providence neighborhoods were defined by uniform socioeconomic conditions and by ethnic/color characteristics. The dominant consumption and status values of society, in the context of historical transformations, ensured that either socioeconomic mobility or decline would take people out of their neighborhoods, unless mechanisms were brought into play that allowed them to remain there. The normative thrust of change that explained socioeconomic and ethnic/color neighborhood development went something like this. First, ethnic neighborhoods were formed as immigrants arrived and all were more or less uniformly poor and powerless, seeking work and a means for sustaining their lives. Then, social and economic heterogeneity emerged as some in the neighborhood gained success while others remained mired in struggle. Economic differentiation defined the possibilities of immigrant life. Next, an ethnic leadership developed, with residents mobilizing to support certain individuals politically, and often economically; in return for this support, patronage was extended. After World War II, urban consumption and investment practices created class-based neighborhoods no longer cemented by any single set of ethnic loyalties. At this point, ethnic leaders moved to the new "elite" neighborhoods, and in general the middle class moved from the old neighborhoods into middle-class suburbs. The working and non-working poor either remained behind in their old, "declining" neighborhoods, or moved into areas they were able to afford where other impoverished people like them also collected. Since the 1960s, gentrification has brought about the most recent phase in neighborhood development, in which the "elite" have begun their move back into the city, displacing the working and non-working poor. To protect their own investment, pockets of professionals have campaigned to "stabilize" their adoptive communities.

One curiously critical element in this matrix has been the availability and the encouragement of mixed housing in the patchwork quilt of the city's neighborhoods. Providence's small scale has meant that the poor and wealthy, young and old, healthy and disabled of a particular ethnic group have been able to remain in their neighborhoods and thus sustain political influence based on ethnically defined territoriality. In this respect, it is no coincidence that (1) governments have targeted neighborhoods as political and economic units either to assist in development plans, or, in some cases, to deliberately ignore, thus assuring their decline; (2) politicians chose to mobilize constituencies around ethnicity to propel themselves into office; and (3) neighborhood residents supported politicians and their governments even when they perceived their personal interests being met through patronage, rather than through the formal bureaucratic structures created to equitably distribute resources.

Manny's helped me define the role of Cape Verdeans in Providence. I had to research the origins, development, and transformation of Cape Verdean Fox Pointers in the context of changing conditions with which they have had to deal in order to learn why Cape Verdeans came to frequent the bar. My method did not take the Cape Verdean identity, neighborhood, or community as given. Instead, I sought the conditions that generated ethnic group, neighborhood, and community identity development. This necessitated a historical analysis of the emergence of the bar and of the neighborhood as "Cape Verdean."

Historical analysis is not the recitation of chronology, one fact after another. Historical analysis here has meant an analytical focus on cultural and social relations locally, as they emerged in coordination with regional and global processes. Coordination here did not mean the interdigitation of cogs of wheels, but the sociocultural and economic relations of diverse populations in interaction. As a result, the objects of study were the *conditions* generating processes of becoming, reproduction, and change, rather than structural and functional relations, stasis, and cor-relations. As conditions changed, so did the nature of ethnic group iden-tity. In discussing Cape Verdean ethnicity, then, it was necessary to discuss the contexts of particular historic conjunctions. Since ethnic group identity was different in each, the symbols available and chosen to help create that identity changed from one period to the next.

As I have tried to show, the Brava Islanders were the most active in whaling, so it was simpler for New Englanders to refer to Cape Verdeans as "Bravas." To a New England Yankee, a Brava was a "Black" whaler. The conditions that brought about this identity were centered in the economy that created a labor force for New England enterprises, the same commercial forces that brought about the settling of the Atlantic Islands off the west coast of Africa. Profit-making and the commoditiza-tion of virtually everything, particularly human labor, drove economic expansion. The expansion of European economies was made possible through the movement of large numbers of people over great distances and their use as inexpensive labor in agrarian enterprises. People were grouped according to ethnicities, which fit, in turn, into a socioeconomic hierarchy in which cultural development (i.e. civilization) was critical in determining the nature of work that members of a particular group would be able to carry out. The capital generated in these forms of speculation provided for further economic experimentation. Shifts in the economy often coincided with the development of new political forms that acted to promote further expansion of the economy and created new contexts for and shifts in group identity development, and so it was with Cape Ver-deans.

As discussed earlier, the shift from recognizably world-wide occupa-tional status to globally effective race/class status was never clear-cut. The value and meaning given to skin color varied at local levels and in relationship to state-level politics. For example, Bravas were often lighter-skinned Cape Verdean whalers, but in the context of Yankees in New England, they were Black and poor. The dominance of one status over another, characterized by unique traits and trait complexes, as a means for classifying groups of people or as a mechanism for self-identity, changed over time and according to context. I have discerned the importance of "class," "race," and "ethnicity" (but also occupation) as significant criteria of group identity only at specific coincidences within historical processes. I could not assume these criteria to be traditional forms and structures of social organization passed on through the genera-tions as traditions because cultural, social, and economic changes would have remained hidden, as would have power relations that constrained or generated changes. As we have seen, the specific identity of a group of people crystallized at given moments in time and constantly changed in relation to political and economic conditions.

European states that experienced transformation, in articulation with societies that supported their own political systems through the payments of tribute, dominated African colonial experiences, expanded their European-centered economies, and integrated them into a world system that was constituted by a division of labor by class, ethnicity, and race. Africans, in particular (but also religious minorities and criminals), were used as an inexpensive slave labor force for the plantation system, whose dimensions grew with the "discovery" of the New World. The Cape Verde Islands played an important role in the transporting of Africans to the Americas. The strategic location of the islands made them an important provisioning depot in this long-distance enterprise. And Cape Verde, like other Atlantic islands, was a prototype for initial plantation experiments that were later transported and expanded into a universal mercantile economy. Much like the Azoreans, the Cape Verdeans became primary sources of labor in the sea trades, particularly after the whaling industry began to flourish in New England.

The commodification of Cape Verdean labor took place at about this time. Although not slaves, the low level of remuneration for Cape Verdeans' work on whaling vessels did not allow their financial emancipation. Much like the southern and eastern Europeans and the Chinese, the Cape Verdeans sought to better their conditions of life by migrating to new and potentially more lucrative sources of work. Their special place within the Portuguese Empire, the light skin color of the Brava Islanders, and what was perceived by employers as their "passive" character were the unique conditions that allowed them to travel and finally settle on New England shores.

While free Africans already were living in Rhode Island when Cape Verdeans resettled from their communities in nearby Massachusetts, most likely it was the availability of work and housing that attracted them to the Ocean State. The structural context of racial prejudice had not been eliminated just because Rhode Islanders had lived through the period of slavery and were among the first to fight against it. Yet race and poor working conditions did not fully coincide, since poverty was experienced among most immigrants, Black and white, who had a poor grasp of English and poor working skills. However, when all else was equal, people of color earned less for their work and tended to obtain only that work rejected by others. Similarly, the choices for housing were limited for all poorly skilled working people, but even more so for people of color. Hence, working poor people were politically segmented by the forces of production that brought them to New England in the first place and defined them ethnically, restricting upward mobility for some but permitting it for others.

As discussed earlier, in Providence these conditions gave rise to the curious settlement pattern of poor working people grouped in ethnic communities along the water's edge, virtually encircling the oldest area of European settlement. This is where Indians, Africans, and Cape Verdeans lived, as well as poor eastern and southern Europeans, the Irish, and other "Portuguese." The density of Cape Verdeans along South Main and neighboring streets was so great that people recognized the Cape Verdean claim that this was "their" neighborhood, and it is here that the notion of Fox Point as a Cape Verdean community was created.

Fox Point, or more specifically South Main Street, attracted Cape Verdeans who had first settled in Massachusetts. They or their parents came from different parts of the Islands and different communities, and became neighbors, friends, and relatives. The Fox Point settlement helped crystallize a Cape Verdean identity created from the diverse island cultural histories of the people who made up the community. Neighborhood, ethnic, and racial identities overlapped to the degree that one category made the others predictable. If you were from Fox Point, you were "Black Portuguese." In addition, as the whaling economy declined and disappeared, waterfront work became the primary occupation of Cape Verdean men. The availability of work through personal networks further integrated Cape Verdeans along ethnic, racial, class, and occupational lines, and out of this context Fox Point Cape Verdean society was further integrated through a sense of community that was expressed as "family."

Until the 1930s, Providence Cape Verdeans were locked into the lowest echelons of the socioeconomic hierarchy, working in the same job areas as African-Americans: the building and construction trades, domestic service, coal shoveling, hauling, and longshoring. Cape Verdeans were able to sustain a virtual monopoly on dock work, while sharing their place on the bottom of society with other racial groups. The competition for resources, particularly scarce jobs, brought about politicization along ethnic and neighborhood lines. The issue of "race," from the dominant American perspective, was simple and rigidly defined, with "white" being on top and "black" on the bottom. The fact that some people of color found upward mobility provided the demonstrable slippage in the system which sustained a dominant ideology that "in

America everyone is equal and race is not a handicap.'' The inequalities that have characterized interethnic, interracial, and inter-class hostilities in America are embedded in the obvious contradiction between power relations and the potential for upward mobility so clearly demonstrated by the experience of the Fox Point Cape Verdeans.

The scarcity of acceptable work brought people from the least well-paid areas of production into competition with each other and in the process created the cultural divisions necessary for the distribution of limited resources along ethnic lines. In this process, the "White Portuguese" rejected the "Black Portuguese," and they, in turn, rejected African-Americans. Cultural traditions such as language, food, and kinship or social relations further separated people economically and politically, disenfranchising groups from each other. Despite similar placement in American society and shared economic disadvantages, the diverse immigrant groups could rarely unify to alter their conditions. Particularly severe industrial crises between 1919 and 1939, though, did bring on a series of strikes and other forms of labor unrest, including the formation of unions. The monopoly of local occupations by certain ethnic groups also led to the creation of labor unions, as in the 1930s, when the Cape Verdeans in Rhode Island (Providence in particular) successfully organized a local Longshoremen's Association whose members to this day sustain a Cape Verdean identity. The irony of ethnically based labor unions was that they struggled against class-based unity in the competition for local resources and power and in the process further segmented the struggle of labor and thus deferred power to the privileged.

World War I reduced the flow of Cape Verdeans to New England. This trend was institutionalized by the new immigration laws of the 1917 through 1922 period, which further reduced Cape Verdean movement across the Atlantic. The decline in the United States economy also did not encourage efforts to increase the migrant labor flow. With no new waves of Cape Verdean Islanders coming to sustain the links between the homeland and the diaspora, Fox Point Cape Verdeans further solidified their insulated position within existing New England social relations. Their cultural separateness thus defined their place in the region and assured their role in the local production process. Their success in forming the Longshoremen's Association in Providence demonstrated the vitality and strength of Cape Verdean ethnicity as a vehicle for local-level political organization.

It was in this context that Manny Almeida's Ringside Lounge came into play as a Cape Verdean bar. The relationship between dock work and Cape Verdean identity remained important, but as Cape Verdeans pursued higher education and higher-status jobs, they could no longer be identified as longshoremen only. That they lived in what most people identified as a "slum" continued to separate them from people who sought better living quarters. Cape Verdeans were stigmatized by their residential area, which government officials feared would diffuse into the wealthy college neighborhood and, like a disease, further spread deterioration and economic decline.

In addition to the fear of an expanding slum, the loss of the healthy middle-class tax base that had brought Providence into prosperity at the turn of the century would further increase the tendency to urban decline. Two contradictory processes were set in motion that ultimately reversed this trend and created the conditions of Cape Verdean displacement. The area's colleges expanded their campuses. Brown University in particular purchased property and demolished buildings to create a new academic environment. The fear that irreplaceable historic buildings would be lost and the memory of the Yankee past would be extinguished brought the Historic Preservation Society into being. Some of the East Side's wealthy and powerful residents were galvanized into action to reverse the destruction of one of America's most historic districts. Federal funds were secured to protect and rehabilitate the esthetically pleasing and historically significant buildings and streets, and the long-standing city plan to renew and develop this section of town was reactivated.

Route 195 cut off Fox Point from the sea and eliminated George M. Cohan Boulevard, a local landmark. Large sections of South Main Street were razed and rebuilt. Benefit and other nearby streets were "preserved," causing prices for housing to skyrocket. The Providence Redevelopment Agency, part of the city government, functioned to accommodate urban renewal by condemning properties and evacuating people from the section of Fox Point to be affected.

A complex set of factors prevented Cape Verdean home ownership in Fox Point. One crucial factor was the increasing cost of housing real estate; the banking practice of not making credit available to particular groups of people or in certain areas was another factor. However, some Cape Verdeans speculated that purchasing real estate was not a part of the Cape Verdean worldview. That is to say, some Fox Point Cape Verdeans believed that their parents did not have a well-developed sense of private ownership of property. While this idea fits well the perspective of community life as a "family," where everything is shared and society is more or less undifferentiated, some Cape Verdeans did come to own houses. A number of others could have afforded to own property, but decided not to invest their money in this manner. Two points are clear. (1)

Fox Point Cape Verdeans, as a group, did not own their own houses because they did not have the money to do so or because it was not seen to be part of what Cape Verdeans ought to do, despite the exceptions. (2) When Cape Verdeans might have wished to invest, they were not allowed this opportunity due to redlining and the other forces that compelled them to move out of their neighborhood.

In any case, no matter what causes and conditions generated the removal, displacement, or migration of Cape Verdeans from Fox Point, whether voluntarily or through political and economic coercion, the point is that Cape Verdeans as a community in Fox Point ceased to exist. This did not mean that their presence ceased to exist in their neighborhood, nor that they stopped thinking of themselves as a community, but it does mean they ceased to function as a residential community. The few who remained behind watched their relatives and friends move out. The homes evacuated by Cape Verdeans were either razed or became housing for the well-to-do. The shops, cafes, and bars that served the working poor and immigrants were turned into establishments for the chic. The poor were displaced by a predominantly white middle class and the neighborhood was transformed.

Fox Point Cape Verdean ethnicity no longer had a material existence when the neighborhood no longer existed for Cape Verdeans who ceased to live there. However, as Manny Almeida's Ringside Lounge demonstrates, Cape Verdeans continued to struggle for their neighborhood by maintaining a presence there, and their identity as "Fox Pointers" has persisted. Only a few individuals consciously perceived their visits to Manny's as a political act. Most Cape Verdeans who came to Manny's came to maintain a connection with their past and with their friends and kin, "to see friends and relatives." At Manny Almeida's Ringside Lounge, memories of a community in which "everyone was family" were allowed to grow into memories of a struggle to keep residences in Fox Point and hence a struggle for their neighborhood and against being dehumanized, displaced, and forgotten.

REFERENCES

Secondary Sources

Almeida, Raymond Anthony, ed.
    1978 *Cape Verdeans in America: Our Story.* Boston: Tchuba; The American Committee for Cape Verde, Inc.

Beck, Sam
    1983 *From Cape Verde to Providence: The International Longshoremen's Association Local 1329.* Providence, RI: Local 1329 Publications.

Brown, Harris, Stevens, Inc.
    1963 *Market and Land Use Analysis: East Side Urban Renewal Area.* Report submitted to the Providence Redevelopment Agency, Providence, RI.

Buhle, Paul
    1983 Introduction. In *A History of Rhode Island Working People.* Paul Buhle et al., eds. Providence, RI: AFL-CIO, pp. iii-iv.

Cabral, Steven and Sam Beck
    1982 *Nha Distino: Cape Verdean Folk Arts.* Providence, RI: Museum of Natural History Publications.

Cadey, John Hutchins
    1957 *The Civic Architectural Development of Providence: 1636-1950.* Providence, RI: The Book Shop.

CETA
    1979 *Fox Point and Its People: A Community Diary.* Videotape documentary funded by CETA, Fox Point Community Organization and the Rhode Island Committee for the Humanities. Mary McKinney, producer and editor; Marianne A. Cocchini, administrative director; and Sam Beck, humanist scholar. Length, 30 minutes, 3/4 inch black and white. Available through the Brown University Media Center.

Dicker, June
1968 *Kinship and Ritual Kinship Among Cape Verdeans in Providence.* MA thesis. Department of Anthropology. Brown University, Providence, RI.

Goering, John Moylan
1968 *Ethnic Consciousness and Political Behavior.* Ph.D. dissertation. Brown University. Providence, RI.

Halter, Marylin
1984 Working in the Cranberry Bogs: Cape Verdeans in Southeastern Massachusetts. In *Spinner: People and Culture in Southeastern Massachusetts.* Vol. III. Donna Huse, ed. New Bedford Spinner Publications.

Halter, Marylin
1986 Cape Verdean-American Immigration: Background and Overview. Paper presented at the Conference on Social Science Research on Contemporary Cape Verde. Praia, São Tiago. October 24-28.

Lyall, Archibald
1938 *Black and White Makes Brown.* London: Reyerson Press.

Machado, Deidre A. Meintell
1978 *Cape Verdean-Americans: Their Cultural and Historical Background.* Ph.D. dissertation. Department of Anthropology. Brown University, Providence, RI.

Mannix, Daniel Pratt
1968 (1962) *Black Cargoes: A History of the Atlantic Slave Trade, 1518-1865.* In collaboration with Malcolm Comley. New York: Viking Press

Mayer, Kurt Bernd and Sidney Goldstein
1958 *Migration and Economic Development in Rhode Island.* Providence, RI: Brown University Press.

Providence Journal
1980 *Portugal-Cape Verde: Special Issue*, May 18, Providence, RI.

Robinson, Cedric J.
1983 *Black Marxism: The Making of the Black Radical Tradition*. London: Zed Press.

Szwed, John F.
1972 (1969) An American Anthropological Dilemma: The Politics of Afro-American Culture. In Dell Hymes, ed. *Reinventing Anthropology*. New York: Pantheon Books, pp. 153-181.

Williams, Eric
1966 (1944) *Capitalism and Slavery*. New York: Capricorn Books.

Primary Sources

1802-1902 *Providence, RI, City Documents, Volumes 1801-1901.*

1934 *Proposed Slum Clearance and Housing Project for Providence: South Main and Wickenden St.*

1935 *Providence City Plan Commission's 21st Annual Report.*

1950 *Tentative Plan for South Main Project Area D8-A.* Providence Redevelopment Agency.

1967 (1959) *College Hill: A Demonstration Study of Historic Area Renewal (Second Edition).* City Plan Commission and HUD Providence, RI: College Hill Press.

Manny Almeida's Ringside Lounge sign, 1980. (Photograph by the author.)

Fox Point in the early 1970s, view to the west toward College Hill. The Brown University Sciences Library tower is in background behind square church steeple. (Photograph courtesy of the Fox Point Community Organization-CETA Project.)

View to the south from Weybosset Bridge, showing the harbor, South Water Street, and Dyer Street, circa 1867. (Photograph RHi x3 1180 courtesy of the Rhode Island Historical Society.)

Vendors and carts on South Water Street early in the morning, 1903.
(Photograph RHi x3 1455 courtesy of the Rhode Island Historical Society.)

South Main Street, view to the south from Power Street, 1951.
(Photograph RHi x3 6083 courtesy of the Rhode Island Historical Society.)

Three boys with bicycle, late 1940s.
(Photograph RHi E 79 12 20 courtesy of the Rhode Island Historical Society.)

Man playing guitar, circa 1945.
(Photograph RHi E79 1052 courtesy of the Rhode Island Historical Society.)

Girl in confirmation dress in front of 36 Wickenden Street, circa 1950.
(Photograph RHi x3 6081 courtesy of the Rhode Island Historical Society.)

European Tobacco Store, with the owner behind the counter, circa 1951.
(Photograph RHi E79 706 courtesy of the Rhode Island Historical Society.)

Willis J. Jones (*left*) and Toy Fernandes on the occasion of the fiftieth anniversary of the International Longshoremen's Association Local 1329. (Photograph by the author.)

George Dias on the occasion of the fiftieth anniversary of the
International Longshoremen's Association Local 1329.
(Photograph by the author.)

Retired members on the occasion of the fiftieth anniversary of
the International Longshoremen's Association Local 1329.
(Photograph by the author.)

In front of Bobby's Bar.

(Photograph RHi E791 165 courtesy of the Rhode Island Historical Society.)

In front of Manny Almeida's Ringside Lounge, early 1970s.
(Photograph courtesy of the Fox Point Community Organization-CETA project.)

Boy sitting on wall, circa 1970
(Photograph courtesy of the Fox Point Community Organization-CETA project.)

In front of the Fox Point Senior High Rise, early 1970s.
(Photograph courtesy of the Fox Point Community Organization-CETA project.)

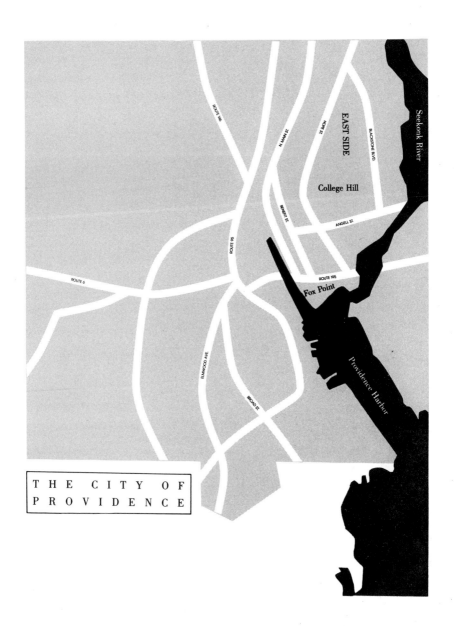

THE CITY OF
PROVIDENCE

EAST SIDE

College Hill

Fox Point

Seekonk River

Providence Harbor

ROUTE 146

N. MAIN ST.

HOPE ST.

BLACKSTONE BLVD.

BENEFIT ST.

ANGELL ST.

ROUTE 95

ROUTE 6

ROUTE 195

ELMWOOD AVE

BROAD ST.

City of Providence

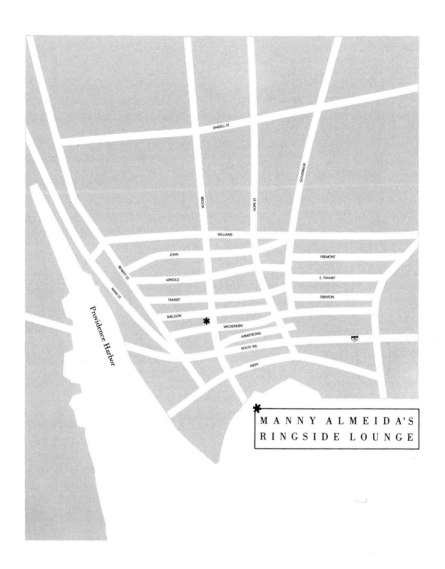

MANNY ALMEIDA'S
RINGSIDE LOUNGE

Fox Point neighborhood